THE
IDIOT

An Interpretation

TWAYNE'S MASTERWORK STUDIES

Robert Lecker, General Editor

THE IDIOT

An Interpretation

VICTOR TERRAS

TWAYNE PUBLISHERS • BOSTON
A Division of G. K. Hall & Co.

Twayne's Masterwork Studies No. 57

Copyright 1990 by G. K. Hall & Co.
All rights reserved.
Published by Twayne Publishers
A division of G. K. Hall & Co.
70 Lincoln Street
Boston, Massachusetts 02111

Copyediting supervised by Barbara Sutton.
Book production by Janet Z. Reynolds.
Typeset in 11/14 Sabon
by Compset, Inc., Beverly, Massachusetts.

First published 1990.
10 9 8 7 6 5 4 3 2 1 (hc)
10 9 8 7 6 5 4 3 2 1 (pbk)

Library of Congress Cataloging-in-Publication Data

Terras, Victor.
    The Idiot, an interpretation / Victor Terras.
        p.   cm. — (Twayne's masterwork studies ; no. 57)
    Includes bibliographical references.
    ISBN 0-8057-9412-3 (alk. paper). — ISBN 0-8057-8133-1 (pbk. :
alk. paper)
        1. Dostoyevsky, Fyodor, 1821–1881. Idiot.   I. Title.
    II. Series.
    PG3325.I33T47   1990
    891.73′3—dc20   90-32544
                                                                CIP

Contents

*Note on the References
and Acknowledgments*

The only authoritative edition of Dostoevsky's works is *Polnoe sobranie sochinenii v tridtsati tomakh* (Leningrad: Nauka, 1972–). Planned in thirty volumes, it is nearly complete. The text of *The Idiot* is in volume 8 of this edition; the notebooks to *The Idiot* are in volume 9. I have used the introductory articles and notes found in this edition in my chapters on critical reception, the notebooks to *The Idiot,* and the literary subtext.

I have used Constance Garnett's translation for my English text (New York: Dell, 1962). I chose Garnett's over other translations given in the Bibliography because her Victorian English is closer to Dostoevsky's Russian than more recent translations. I also feel it is the best translation from a stylistic point of view.

Parenthetic references to the text of *The Idiot* give the page number(s) of the English text first and then those of the Russian edition (i.e., 420/315). All references to the notebooks are my translations of the Russian edition.

The secondary literature on Dostoevsky, and on *The Idiot* in particular, is massive. A small fraction of it was used in this study. Only a few of the most important Russian studies have been identified in the bibliography and are referred to in the text.

Lithograph of Fyodor Dostoevsky by V. D. Falileev, 1921.

Chronology:
Fyodor Dostoevsky's Life and Works

1821   Fyodor Mikhailovich Dostoevsky born in Moscow 30 October, the second son of Mikhail Andreevich Dostoevsky, a doctor in charge of the gynecological ward of the Moscow Marian Hospital for the Poor.

1837   His mother, a gentle and pious woman, dies.

1837–1843   Attends the School for Military Engineers in St. Petersburg, where he is a good student. A voracious reader, he is a loner, respected but not liked by his classmates.

1839   His father dies in June of a stroke, according to the official death certificate. There are rumors that he was murdered by the peasants of his country estate.

1843–1844   After graduation, assigned to the Corps of Engineers in the rank of lieutenant and works as a draftsman, still in St. Petersburg. Resigns his commission, having decided to become a professional writer. His first effort, a translation of Balzac's *Eugénie Grandet,* appears that year.

1845   Finishes his first novel, *Poor Folk,* a sophisticated parody of the sentimental epistolary novel and trenchant psychological study of poverty as a congenital, chronic, and contagious disease. The critic Vissarion Belinsky, on reading the manuscript, hails him as "a new Gogol."

1846   *Poor Folk* appears in *A Petersburg Miscellany,* an almanac. His second novel, *The Double,* appears in the journal *National Annals* only a few weeks after *Poor Folk.* (A critical and public failure in 1846, *The Double* has received inordinate attention in the twentieth century because of its psychological subtleties, intricate structure, and puzzling plot.) Makes the acquaintance of Mikhail Butashevich-Petrashevsky (1821–66), who has a library of prohibited books and holds at his residence regular meetings of a circle of young men interested in utopian socialism.

1847–1849   Establishes himself as a foremost writer of the young generation, publishing a series of stories in the *National Annals*. The first installments of *Netochka Nezvanova*, planned as a full-length novel, appear in the *National Annals*.

1849   Is arrested 23 April with some thirty other members of Petrashevsky's circle and is interned at St. Peter and Paul Fortress. On 22 December he and other members of the circle are taken to Semyonovsky Square and subjected to a mock execution, the condition under which Czar Nicholas I commuted their death sentences. On 24 December starts his journey to Omsk, Siberia, where he serves four years at hard labor in a military prison.

1854   Is released from prison 15 February and a month later is taken under guard to Semipalatinsk in Central Asia, where he serves as a private in a regiment of the line.

1857   Soon to be promoted to officer's rank (March) and to have his status as nobleman restored (May), marries Marya Dmitrievna Isaeva, a young widow, 7 February. Their married bliss is marred by money worries and Dostoevsky's epileptic fits, the first of which probably occurred in prison.

1859   Resigns his commission in May and is allowed to return to European Russia, initially to Tver and then to St. Petersburg. Resumes his literary career.

1861   Starts with his brother Mikhail the literary journal *Vremya* (Time), which has considerable success. His novels *The Insulted and Injured* (1861) and *Notes from the House of the Dead* (1861–62), a fictionalized account of his years in prison, contribute to this success. Also publishes a series of politically conservative articles.

1862   On 7 June starts his first trip to Western Europe, which leads to *Winter Notes on Summer Impressions* (1863), a witty and perceptive travelogue.

1863   *Vremya* is suspended 24 May for having printed an article that authorities interpret as supportive of the cause of the current Polish insurrection.

1863–1865   Begins relationship with Apollinaria Suslova (1840–1918), a minor writer and the prototype of his headstrong, rebellious, and unhappy heroines, such as Nastasya Filippovna of *The Idiot*.

1864   Dostoevsky brothers are given permission to resume publication of their journal under a new title, *Epokha* (Epoch). Marya Dostoevsky dies 15 April; Mikhail Dostoevsky dies 10 July. *Notes from Underground*, philosophically the most challenging of Dostoevsky's works, appears in *Epokha*.

1864–1865   Begins an abortive romance with Anna Korvin-Krukovsky (1843–87), a contributor to *Epokha* and the prototype of Aglaya in *The Idiot*.

1865   Is forced to stop publication of *Epokha*, goes bankrupt, and is hounded by creditors. Pressed for time by a contract to deliver a novel to his publisher, hires a stenographer and dictates to her a short novel, *The Gambler*.

1866   Begins work on his novel *Crime and Punishment*, published serially in the *Russian Herald*, 1866–67.

1867   Marries his stenographer, twenty-year-old Anna Grigoryevna Snitkina, 15 February. Goes abroad with his bride 14 April, mostly to escape creditors. In Germany his financial condition goes from bad to worse as a result of his compulsive gambling. In Geneva, 14 September, makes the first notebook entry toward a novel that will become *The Idiot*.

1867–1871   Lives with Anna in Germany, Switzerland, Italy, Austria, and again Germany.

1868–1869   *The Idiot* is published serially in the *Russian Herald*.

1869   Finishes *The Idiot* in Florence 17 January.

1871   Returns to St. Petersburg 9 June.

1871–1872   *The Possessed*, Dostoevsky's strongest antinihilist novel, is published serially in the *Russian Herald*.

1873–1874   Becomes editor in chief of the conservative weekly

Grazhdanin (The Citizen), for which he writes the column "Diary of a Writer."

1875   *A Raw Youth* appears in the *National Annals.*

1876–1881   Independently publishes "Diary of a Writer," a series of miscellaneous essays, articles, reviews, reportage, and short fiction.

1879–1880   *The Brothers Karamazov* appears in the *Russian Herald.*

1880   Delivers his celebrated "Discourse on Pushkin" in Moscow 8 June.

1881   Dies in St. Petersburg 28 January of a pulmonary hemorrhage after having suffered from emphysema for several years.

1

Historical Context

The Idiot is about Russia's young generation in the late 1860s. Dostoevsky wrote this novel when enthusiasm over the liberal reforms of Alexander II was beginning to wane, while their effects were proving to be irreversible. The abolition of serfdom (in Russian, *krepostnoe pravo*, from *krepost'*, "deed" and *pravo*, "law," the legal principle by which a peasant was tied to the land of its holder) in 1861 and subsequent reforms of judicial, civil, and military administrations had created the legal basis for a modern *Rechtsstaat* and a capitalist society. Postreform Petersburg, where the action of *The Idiot* unfolds, was a modern metropolis. Its industrial plants and financial institutions were no different from Europe's. Fortunes were made and lost on the St. Petersburg stock exchange. Money was the dominant power. The Russian legal system was definitely Western, including even trial by jury in criminal cases. As a result, the legal profession was rapidly gaining in importance, self-assurance, and prestige. With government control over the universities relaxed and students flocking to the classes of "progressive" professors, particularly in the natural sciences, a positivist and

materialist worldview was becoming the norm among the educated. Russia's progress was perceived by most in terms of
scientific, industrial, and educational emulation of Western
standards. With censorship also relaxed, journalism of all political persuasions and modes—from responsible to sensational,
from semiofficial to yellow—flourished, attracting many of the
best minds and pens but also many irresponsible and semiliter-
ate scribblers.

The call for a woman's right to a free choice of her marriage
partner, to a higher education, and to a vocation was high on
the agenda of Russian progressives. Educated young women ac-
tively participated in their organizations, journals, and literary
projects. With the erosion of the patriarchal family structure,
the Russian family ceased being a bulwark of the existing social
order. There arose what Dostoevsky called the "accidental
family."

The radicalism and nihilism of the young *shestidesyatniki*
(from *shest'desyat,* "sixty," hence "men of the sixties") were
quite unprecedented in Russia. Cruelly disappointed that the reforms of the early 1860s had not produced a better society,
some young intellectuals turned to organized subversion and violence. In 1866 Dmitry Karakozov, a student, made an attempt
on the czar's life. Subsequently there were more plots, and Alexander II was eventually assassinated in 1881. Other young people renounced their ideals and turned cynical and selfish.

All of these phenomena generated concern among conservative Russians, like Dostoevsky. These concerns are reflected
rather directly in *The Idiot* and Dostoevsky's other novels of the
1860s and 1870s. Since his return to the literary world in 1860
Dostoevsky was the leader of a group identified as *pochva,* "the
soil," or *pochvenniki,* "men of the soil," who rejected the legal-
ism, scientism, and positivism of the progressives as imports
from the West that were alien to the spirit of the Russian people
and interfered with Russia's "organic" development. Other
pochvenniki were Apollon Grigoryev (1822–64) and Nikolai

Strakhov (1828–96), both contributors to *Vremya,* the journal of the Dostoevsky brothers. To Dostoevsky and the other *pochvenniki,* the Russian progressives—liberals or radicals—were "theoreticians" who in the pursuit of their secondhand ideas ignored Russian reality.

Against the ideas of liberal and radical progressives, Dostoevsky opposed his own ideas of a resurgent Russia rising on the strength of its own cultural traditions and spiritual resources. Like the Slavophiles, with whom he agreed on many but also disagreed on a few issues, Dostoevsky felt that Western civilization was in decline and would be regenerated by Russian spirituality if the educated Russian elite found a way back to the Christian faith of the simple Russian people.

The basic points of Dostoevsky's position were close to that of the Slavophiles. He refused to judge Russia by Western standards, believing that Russian values were not the same: Western-style parliamentary democracy and competitive individualism were alien to a Russian mentality, which was more inclined toward an authoritarian monarchy and voluntary communal endeavor. (Westernizers such as Ivan Turgenev considered this position "nonsense and swinishness.") Although not rejecting science or progress through science, Dostoevsky and other *pochvenniki,* along with the Slavophiles, insisted that science should rise to the challenge of faith in a positive way and not negate faith. In the case of a conflict between faith and science, they would follow faith.

The conflict between progressives and *pochvenniki* could be reduced to their respective image of the Russian people. Progressives saw the people as basically materialist, irreverent, and areligious. Dostoevsky saw them as devoutly religious, gifted with a deep spirituality, and inclined to respect authority. To progressives, liberal or radical, the Russian people needed to be educated and enlightened. To Dostoevsky, it was the westernized elite that had to learn humbly to follow the example of the people.

The conservative—or reactionary—utopia that was on Dostoevsky's mind had a long tradition in Russia. Prince M. M. Shcherbatov (1733–90), M. M. Kheraskov (1733–1807), A. D. Ulybyshev (1794–1858), Prince V. F. Odoevsky (1803–69), and I. V. Kireevsky (1806–56), among others, had imagined a world in which the ways of a technically and socially sophisticated urban society based on rational principles had failed and the ways of a patriarchal rural community had prevailed. Dostoevsky's own utopian dreams and eschatological fears followed this tradition. A golden age of innocence associated with a serene classical landscape (similar to that in *Acis and Galatea,* a painting by Claude Lorrain that Dostoevsky had seen in a Dresden museum) was a permanent feature of his mind. It appears in the notebooks to *The Idiot* and repeatedly in his published works (in the chapter "At Tikhon's" of *The Possessed,* in *A Raw Youth,* and in "Dream of a Ridiculous Man"). The image of an inner, spiritual Arcadia, which allows a man to lead a selfless, serene, life-affirming existence amid the turmoil of a sinful and strife-ridden contemporary world, is another fixture of Dostoevsky's imagination. Each of Dostoevsky's major novels features at least one character like Prince Myshkin of *The Idiot* whose inner world is paradisiacally pure. It is significant that we meet Dostoevsky's last heroes, Father Zosima and Alyosha Karamazov, in a monastery. Prince Myshkin, too, has some traits that suggest monastic life.

The hero of Dostoevsky's spiritual utopia is the opposite of the brash, efficient, materialist heroes of the progressives, such as the successful businessman Stoltz in *Oblomov* (1859), by Ivan Goncharov, a liberal, or the self-confident, resourceful, and practical "new man" of the radical Nikolai Chernyshevsky's phenomenally successful novel *What Is to Be Done?* (1863). In Dostoevsky's works, these types are invariably presented as negative and are usually defeated in the end. Dostoevsky's *pochvennik* friend, the poet and critic Apollon Grigoryev, had said that Russia's future belonged not to the "grasping" Westernized, but to the "meek" native Russian, whose prototype he believed to have recognized in the humble title character of Aleksandr Pushkin's *Tales of the Late Ivan Petrovich Belkin* (1831). Dostoevsky's real heroes and heroines are Christians—poor, meek, short on worldly success, but strong in faith. Such had been the Marmeladovs, father and daughter, in *Crime and Punishment.* Such are Prince Myshkin and the Swiss shepardess Marie in *The Idiot.* The pattern became even more pronounced in the following novels.

Dostoevsky was not, however, intent on preaching an entirely otherworldly message. There is an effort in each of Dostoevsky's major novels to juxtapose the negative types of liberal or radical men of action against his own energetic conservative activists. But these tend to be marginal to the action of the novel or very young and thus belonging to the future rather than to the present. This is true of *The Idiot,* where Prince Myshkin's friend, young Kolya Ivolgin, "promises to become an active and useful man."

2

The Importance of the Work

Dostoevsky had a stronger than usual personal commitment to *The Idiot*. He struggled with expressing its theme more arduously than he had in any other work and felt that he had not altogether succeeded in his endeavor. But the idea of a "perfectly beautiful human being" cast into contemporary Russian society was dear to his heart, and he insisted that although he would not necessarily defend his work, he certainly would stand behind its idea. Dostoevsky's fondness for *The Idiot* also can be explained by the fact that he put more of himself, and more of his better self, into the character of its hero than he ever had in any of his other works.

As far as the hero of the novel is concerned, *The Idiot* is at worst a heroic attempt to introduce a Christ figure into a thoroughly secular and sinful modern world, and thus deserving of a succès d'estime; at best it is one of the few works in all literature where such an attempt met with success.

Ippolit Terentyev, Prince Myshkin's ideological antagonist, develops a theme that accompanied Dostoevsky from *Poor Folk* to *The Brothers Karamazov*. That theme is the apparent incompatibility of the condition of this world, whose principal trait is that in it everything and everybody must die, with the notion that this world is the creation of a God who is all powerful, all good, and all loving. A string of encounters with death is subtly woven into the texture of the novel, developing the pros and cons of Ippolit's argument. Ippolit, a seventeen-year-old dying of consumption, is one of Dostoevsky's great devil's advocates, both by virtue of his own fate and by that of the power of his impassioned protest against the condition of this world as he, an unbeliever, sees it.

Although Prince Myshkin may or may not be a successful incarnation of Dostoevsky's idea and may or may not refute Ippolit's argument, it is a fact that *The Idiot* is populated by more fascinating, memorable, and credible characters than any other novel by Dostoevsky except *The Brothers Karamazov*. Nastasya Filippovna and Parfyon Rogozhin are great tragic figures, supported by a strong cast of male and female characters, several of whom are deeply interesting in their own right. They are drawn against a broad panorama of life on several levels of Petersburg society: the upper-middle-class world of the Epanchins, hardly different from its equivalent in the West, the lower-middle-class world of the Lebedevs and Ptitsyns, somewhat less Western, the gloomy old-fashioned Russian world of the Rogozhins, and the motley crowd of various déclassé types such as the Ivolgins, Kellers, and Burdovskys.

The Idiot is a socially and psychologically intriguing novel featuring several characters with neuroses that reflect social problems of universal interest. Rogozhin's tragedy mirrors the ambience of the Russian merchant class in which acquisition and possession are the main forms assumed by human relations. The self-destructive behavior of Nastasya Filippovna, which in a milder form also appears in Aglaya Epanchina, projects the plight of an energetic, intelligent, and highly self-conscious woman whom society denies any role but that established by convention. Ganya Ivolgin, likewise self-destructive, is the victim of a society that above all prizes individual success, but withholds from those who aspire for it anywhere near an equal chance to attain it. His father, a cashiered general, is a profound study in the moral and mental deterioration that afflicts a man deprived of his position in society. Several other characters—such as Lebedev, Keller, and Mme Epanchina—are of almost equal interest.

The Idiot features some of Dostoevsky's most energetic writing. The whole of part 1 and the concluding chapters of part 4, in particular, manage to sustain an energy level rarely matched in all of nineteenth-century literature. The novel has an extraordinarily large number of individualized characters, exciting scenes, provocative thoughts, and vivid descriptions, all of which are made palpable by Dostoevsky's great forte, concreteness of detail. In The Idiot, Dostoevsky's other source of energy—speech that is energized by individualization, irony, ambiguity, or parody—is utilized less than in his other major novels. The narrative voice is an ordinary one, though the narrator occasionally assumes the viewpoint of one of the characters or of the public at large, usually with sardonic irony. The dialogue, though, is dramatically effective throughout and often brilliant. There are some great scenes: "duels," such as the meeting of Aglaya and Nastasya Filippovna, and "conclaves," in which most of the cast gathers to generate suspense, excitement, turmoil, surprise revelations, and outrageous actions, such as at Nastasya Filippovna's nameday party in part 1.

The Idiot has all the makings of a great novel: a profound philosophic conception vigorously developed, a cast of characters who are both fascinating and robustly alive, a vigorous plot that leads up to one of the great finales in all literature, and pages upon pages of strong writing. It lacks, however, the presence of a personalized narrative voice, which so enhances the palpable immediacy of the action in The Possessed, A Raw Youth, and The Brothers Karamazov. It is on account of this failing that some critics have denied The Idiot the greatness of The Possessed or The Brothers Karamazov.

3

Critical Reception

The Idiot was no great hit with the public, and immediate critical reactions were generally negative, a likely response in light of the political situation. Dostoevsky bore by then the unequivocal label of conservative, and the aura of his martyrdom had worn thin. A majority of his reviewers were political opponents, either liberal or radical, and approached his work intending to discredit it. Even the few conservative reviewers had no reason to be overly enthusiastic, for Dostoevsky's conservative message was tainted by some nasty digs at high society, the business world, and the merchant class.

A point that was made by many reviewers was that the novel was "fantastic," unrelated to the real world. D. I. Minaev (1835–89), a radical, wrote: "This is a fairy tale in which 'the more improbable' means 'the better.' People meet, become acquainted, fall in love, slap each other's face—and all at the author's first whim, without any artistic truth. Millions of inherited money fly about in the novel like so many bouncing balls."[1] Minaev, a talented parodist, added some ironic verses lampooning the novel. V. P. Burenin (1841–1926), a liberal, responded to successive installments of *The Idiot* three times in the *St. Petersburg News*,[2] each time negatively. He called the novel "utterly hopeless," the presentation of the young generation unfair ("the purest fruit of the novelist's subjective fancy"), and the whole novel "a belletristic compilation, concocted from a multitude of absurd personages and events, without any concern for any kind of artistic objectivity." Burenin, like other reviewers, was particularly angry at Dostoevsky's portrayal of the young nihilists:

> Young people, as presented in *The Idiot*, are some kind of a gang, comprised of morally deranged youths. All of these young people writhe and warp, some from self-love, others from the baseness of their souls, and some, finally, simply from physical ailments; all of them speak as if they were delirious, the author forces all of them to act neurotically, with the secret intent of disgracing some of their aspirations which are obviously unwelcome to the author. (no. 53)

E. L. Markov (1835–1903), a liberal novelist and critic, agreed: "This pervasive nightmare, bearing little similarity to real life, lacks any of the colors of life, any of its soothing aspects, and in it the contemplations and confessions of a psychiatric patient moan in a stubbornly monotonous tone."[3]

A charge—one Dostoevsky had heard as early as at the appearance of *The Double* in 1846—was advanced time and again—that his characters were all psychopaths and hence irrelevant to the real world of normal people. Nikolai Leskov (1831–95), himself a great writer and ideologically not that far removed from Dostoevsky, reviewed *The Idiot* anonymously and observed that "all of the acting characters of the novel, as if on purpose, are afflicted with mental illnesses." Leskov, however, correctly defined the author's idea as one according to which the qualities of Prince Myshkin (ingenuousness, righteousness, simplicity, accompanied by "a profound understanding of the human soul") are the means toward the attainment of any kind of private or social goals.[4]

Dostoevsky's novels, and *The Idiot* in particular, met with an early appreciation on the part of Vladimir Chizh, a Moscow psychiatrist, who published *Dostoevsky as Psychopathologist* (1885), in which he pointed out that Dostoevsky's description of an epileptic seizure in *The Idiot* was so accurate it was valuable even to a clinical psychiatrist. In line with the crass positivism of his age, Chizh went on to suggest that Myshkin's tragedy rested with the unhealthy life-style to which he was exposed and the inadequate medical care given him.

The most important contemporary reaction to *The Idiot* came from Mikhail Saltykov-Shchedrin (1826–89), a writer and critic of the first rank, who was a leader of the radicals and Dostoevsky's lifelong adversary. In a review of I. V. Fyodorov-Omulevsky's novel *Step by Step,* Saltykov-Shchedrin also got around to discussing *The Idiot.* He conceded that Dostoevsky's ultimate goals were the same as those of the progressive circles of Russian society, saying that his "attempt to depict a type of man who had attained full moral and spiritual equilibrium" was a goal of utmost importance. But then Saltykov-Shchedrin goes on to ask, "But what do we see? In spite of the shining beauty of his goal ... Mr. Dostoevsky quite unabashedly undermines his own cause, as he paints a most disgraceful picture of the very people whose efforts are entirely directed at the very objective apparently pursued by him."[5] Saltykov-Shchedrin then elaborates on this apparent "profound contradiction": "All this covers Mr. Dostoevsky's works with spots that are entirely inappropriate to them, and side by side with pictures which testify to his high artistic perceptiveness, it produces scenes indicative of an entirely too immediate and superficial understanding of life and its phenomena. ... On the one hand ... there appear characters full of life and truth, but on the other, some kind of mysterious puppets hopping about as though in a dream, made by hands that were trembling with rage."[6] Altogether then, contemporaries treated *The Idiot* as yet another "anti-nihilist" novel of "the Katkov school."

Orest Miller (1833–89), an academic scholar, made some valuable observations in his "Public Lectures."[7] He likened Prince Myshkin to Johnny the Fool (*Ivanushka durachok*) of the Russian folktale, a character who is not in his right mind, who cannot stand the sight of someone else suffering, and who keeps forgetting himself for the sake of others. (Miller was a noted folklorist.) He thus laid the foundation to an allegoric or symbolic interpretation of the novel. Miller also connected the Swiss episode in *The Idiot* with Tolstoi's story "Lucerne," set in Switzerland, and pointed out that both declare that true freedom and true humanity are not guaranteed by any "liberal code" but must be ingrained in man's inner being. Finally, Miller suggested that Prince Myshkin's Slavophile tirades did not fit his psychological profile at all—probably a just observation.

Symbolist critics of the 1890s and 1900s, such as A. L. Volynsky (1863–1926), D. S. Merezhkovsky (1865–1941), and Vyacheslav Ivanov (1866–1949), all under the influence of Friedrich Nietzsche, tended to interpret *The Idiot* in terms of myth and prophecy. Volynsky, in *Dostoevsky* (St. Petersburg: 1st ed. 1906, 2d ed. 1909), saw Nastasya Filippovna as an incarnation of the Eternal Feminine: satanic forces seek to possess and humiliate the Russian beauty, but because she is childlike and pure at heart, she will at last be saved. Prince Myshkin, the godman (a term taken from the mystic philosophy of Vladimir Solovyov [1853–1900], who in turn took it from the German mystic Jakob Boehme), is a savior who helps her to overcome her dark and violent bacchic impulses. Volynsky's interpretation is vitiated by his reading into the novel "nightmarish orgiastic drinking sprees and bacchanalia" that are not in the text.

To Merezhkovsky, Dostoevsky was the prophet of Russia's religious revolution, as he sought to demonstrate in *Prophet of the Russian Revolution* (1906). Prince Myshkin was, according to Merezhkovsky, a man of "the city that is yet to come," while the other members of the cast are denizens of the existing city, Petrine Russia.

The great symbolist poet Vyacheslav Ivanov was a lifelong devotee of Dostoevsky. He synthesized his several essays on Dostoevsky in the German-language *Dostojewskij* (Tübingen: J. C. B. Mohr, 1932), better known under its English title, *Freedom and the Tragic Life: A Study in Dostoevsky*. To Ivanov, "Prince Myshkin is first and foremost a descending hero, possessing a spirituality directed toward the earth—he is spirit incarnate, rather than man ascending to the spiritual." Also, Myshkin is guided by a mysterious platonic anamnesis, which makes him both a fool and a wise seer among men who lack this gift. Myshkin's tragedy is that he fails in his quest to win earth (Aglaya) over to the spirit and instead is pulled down to earth by her. Nastasya Filippovna alone recognizes the heavenly angel in him. Ivanov did, however, see in *The Idiot* a contamination of different myths.

Konstantin Mochulsky (1892–1948) synthesized the interpretations of the symbolist critics in his *Dostoevsky: His Life and Works* (1947). Mochulsky distinguishes between an empirical and a metaphysical plane in the novel's meaning. On the empirical plane, Nastasya Filippovna is merely a "proud beauty" and a "wronged heart." On the metaphysical plane, she is the "icon of pure beauty," seduced by the "ruler of this world" and "waiting in her dungeon for her liberator." Nastasya Filippovna is an incarnation of beautiful Psyche of the classical myth, the soul who fell away from God. Having grown proud of her divine beauty, which made her godlike, Psyche uses her freedom for evil, affirming herself in "selfness." Psyche, however, has preserved memories of her heavenly origin, which cause her a feeling of fatal guilt. A man comes to her with tidings about her heavenly home. He recognizes in her the "icon of pure beauty" and feels an affinity for her, as they are both on earth visitors from another world.

The symbolist interpretations of *The Idiot* are all somewhat farfetched and require a liberal and imaginative reading of the text. A new reading in terms of myth and anamnesis has been recently attempted by Roger B. Anderson in *Dostoevsky: Myths of Duality* (1986).

The symbolist readings of *The Idiot* were challenged by A. P. Skaftymov (1890–1968), a Soviet scholar who produced the first monographic study of the novel, "The Thematic Composition of *The Idiot.*"[8] Skaftymov read *The Idiot* as a psychological novel of great analytic depth and social significance. His study is still among the best devoted to *The Idiot*.

The early response to *The Idiot* in the West was mixed. French and English translations appeared in 1887, and the German translation in 1889. The French translation by Victor Derély had a preface by E.-M. de Vogüé, whose seminal work *Le roman russe* had appeared a year earlier. De Vogüé was critical of the novel's composition, a common complaint of Dostoevsky's Western critics: "The plot is started artfully and with verve, the main personages are introduced on the first few pages; but soon they are enveloped by a fantastic mist and get lost in innumerable digressions." Nevertheless, de Vogüé found that the novel had some scenes whose tragic effect matched the tragic scenes of *Othello* or *Macbeth* and that the finale of the novel was "perhaps the most heart-wrenching piece ever written by Dostoevsky." *The Idiot* was much appreciated by several major French writers around the turn of the century, such as Charles-Louis Philippe, Romain Rolland, Octave Mirbeau, André Gide, and others. It has been pointed out that possible echoes from *The Idiot* are found in works by Joris-Karl Huysmans and Georges Bernanos.

The British reception of *The Idiot* was initially negative. Only after the appearance of Constance Garnett's new translation in 1913 did this change. D. H. Lawrence called *The Idiot* his favorite novel by Dostoevsky. Echoes from *The Idiot* have been discovered in works by Hugh Walpole, Joseph Conrad, Henry Sidgwick, and others. The initial reaction to *The Idiot* was also negative in Germany, which possibly was under the influence of Russian critics. In Germany, too, however, *The Idiot* is said to have left traces in the works of major writers such as Jakob Wassermann, Bernhard Kellermann, and Gerhart Hauptmann.

More recent Western criticism of *The Idiot* shows a clear dichotomy between critics who are ready to accept Dostoevsky's religious message and those who are not. Among the former are the German theologian Romano Guardini, the Swiss theologian Walter Nigg, and the American scholar Roger L. Cox. Among the latter, the American scholar Murray Krieger stands out with "Dostoevsky's *Idiot:* The Curse of Saintliness."[9] Krieger's view, according to which Dostoevsky's artistic tact caused him to let his saintly hero bring nothing but death and misery to those whose life he touched, has been restated in various forms, by Michael J. Holquist and Dennis P. Slattery, for example. Most recently, a number of scholarly studies on the structure and style of *The Idiot* have done much to settle the question, raised by Dostoevsky himself, whether *The Idiot* is a work that is in some ways unfinished and deficient. The studies by Robin F. Miller and Brigitte Schultze stand out among many other worthy efforts. Psychoanalytic and psychopathological treatments of Dostoevsky and his works, such as Elizabeth Dalton's *Unconscious Structure in* The Idiot: *A Study in Literature and Psychoanalysis* and James L. Rice's *Dostoevsky and the Healing Art: An Essay in Literary and Medical History,* have undoubtedly affected the reading of *The Idiot* even by those who do not put much stock in these approaches to Dostoevsky's fiction.

Several early attempts to adapt *The Idiot* to the stage failed, largely because of difficulties with the censors, who found the subject too strident and negative for the theater. A stage version of *The Idiot* finally was cleared in 1899 and opened at the Moscow Maly Theater on 11 October and at the St. Petersburg Aleksandrinsky on 4 November. Prominent actors and actresses were eager to have parts in both theaters. At the Aleksandrinsky, M. G. Savina and V. F. Komissarzhevskaya, both great stars, were Nastasya Filippovna and Aglaya. This version remained a part of the Russian repertory even after the Revolution and until World War II. In 1957 G. V. Tovstonogov, one of Russia's leading directors, made a new production of *The Idiot* a gala event on the stage of the Leningrad Bolshoi Dramatic Theater. Since then, *The Idiot* has been staged in many theaters all over the Soviet Union.

Dramatized versions of *The Idiot* have been staged in France, England, Germany, and the United States since the 1920s. Among several versions staged in the English-speaking countries, Robert Montgomery's *Subject to Fits: A Response to Dostoevsky's* The Idiot, which opened in New York on 14 February 1971, was probably the most successful.

The Idiot has been made into a film both in Russia and in the West. A French film of 1946 (by Georges Lampin) and a Japanese film of 1950 (by Akira Kurosawa) are the most memorable.

A Reading

4

The Notebooks to
The Idiot

The Idiot appeared in twelve installments in the *Russian Herald,* a conservative literary journal, from January through December 1868, with no installment in March and a special issue added to no. 12. The novel then appeared as a book in 1874, with some corrections and stylistic changes by the author. Some of Dostoevsky's preparatory materials for *The Idiot* were first published in 1931 under the editorship of P. N. Sakulin and N. F. Belchikov and are now volume 9 of the Academy edition of Dostoevsky's *Collected Works.* An English translation, with commentary, was published by Edward Wasiolek in 1968. The earliest entry is dated 14 September 1867 in Geneva, the last 11 November 1868, probably in Milan. The novel was finished in Florence on 17 January 1869.

Dostoevsky's preparatory materials, usually called notebooks, are interesting for several reasons. They allow us a peek into Dostoevsky's creative laboratory, and let us identify some of his sources and prototypes. They are a valuable aid in the interpretation of his works, since the writer's intent sometimes becomes apparent from his notes and drafts.

Two stages may be observed in Dostoevsky's work on *The Idiot*. The first produced a series of plans (eight at least), random thoughts, and character and plot sketches, all more or less futile and soon rejected. The second led directly to the writing of the novel. It was started in December 1867. Dostoevsky sent the first installment to his publisher, Mikhail Katkov, on 24 December 1867. Dostoevsky's notebooks tell us that he had difficulties in the preparatory stage but that he made remarkably rapid progress once he began writing. We know from Anna Grigoryevna Dostoevsky's memoirs that it took her husband only twenty-three days to write the first seven chapters of part 1. Dostoevsky said the same in a letter to his niece Sofya Ivanova.

The notebooks to *The Idiot* suggest some carryover from preceding works, *Crime and Punishment* and *The Gambler* in particular, much as subsequent works, *The Possessed, A Raw Youth,* and *The Brothers Karamazov,* have a carryover from *The Idiot* and the notebooks to it. Thus, Alyosha Karamazov is identical with Prince Myshkin in the early drafts of *The Brothers Karamazov.* The notebooks tell us that Dostoevsky planned for many years to write a novel about children. This plan was partly realized in several novels, including *The Idiot.*

The notebooks suggest some interesting literary connections. The emerging heroine, who later becomes Nastasya Filippovna, is initially called Mignon, after a character in Goethe's novel *Wilhelm Meisters Lehrjahre,* Aglaya is Hero, apparently after a character in Shakespeare's *Much Ado about Nothing.* Don Quixote is repeatedly mentioned as a prototype of the hero. The great chain of being, a key concept that dominates Tolstoi's *War and Peace,* a work Dostoevsky was reading at the time, shows up in the notes repeatedly. Apparently Dostoevsky saw the antinomy between the goodwill of an individual, Prince Myshkin, and the inexorable flow of the chain of being as a theme of his novel.

Several explicit comments found in the notes relate to the intended moral meaning of the novel. There is, for instance, this entry: "NB NB *The main idea of the novel:* So much power, so much passion in the generation of today, yet they believe in nothing. Boundless idealism together with boundless sensualism" (166). This is valuable evidence to the effect that Dostoevsky saw *The Idiot* as a social novel. Another entry reads: "The main task: The Idiot's character. Develop it. Here is the idea of the novel. How Russia is reflected in him" (252). This suggests that Myshkin was meant to be a symbolic figure standing for Russia as a nation. (This intention is only partly realized in the novel.) Perhaps the most revealing comment is this: "NB. The Prince barely *touched* their lives. But *that* which he could do and undertake, *that* all died with him. *Russia acted upon him gradually. His visions.* But whenever he did *touch* someone, he left an indelible trace everywhere" (242). In another entry this point is specified: "He restores Nastasya Filippovna and acts on Rogozhin by his influence. He causes Aglaya to become more human and takes the General's wife to the point of reverent devotion to him" (252). These entries give a direct answer to those critics who have suggested that Prince Myshkin is an isolated figure who leaves no trace in the world around him or in fact adversely affects the lives of those whose path he crosses.

It was Dostoevsky's habit to jot down editorial comments addressed to himself, often hortative in nature. These entries allow us to understand his attitude toward the writer's craft. For instance, he tells himself, "Write in terms of nothing but facts" (235). We know from Anna Grigoryevna that "fact" (in Russian, *fakt*) was one of her husband's favorite words. He believed that his works were essentially a reflection of the facts of Russian life as perceived by an artist of genius. The following entry is valuable evidence of Dostoevsky's view of reality: "Reality above all. To be sure, maybe we have a different view of reality. 1000 souls. Prophecies—fantastic reality. Maybe in the Idiot man is more real" (276). This entry is reflected in a somewhat obscure passage at the beginning of part 4, chapter 9, whose point is that reality as seen by Dostoevsky may appear fantastic to the reader but that he firmly believes in its basic soundness. Dostoevsky would state this thought more explicitly in the preface to *The Brothers Karamazov*. "1000 souls" is an allusion to Aleksei Pisemsky's novel *One Thousand Souls*, a typical example of solid critical realism. This particular connection is confirmed by the text of the novel. On page 194 (139) there appears a merchant by the name of Papushin. In Pisemsky's novel a merchant named Papushkin plays a fairly significant role.

A marginal note related to Aglaya says, "More gracefully, more ardor, like Princess Katya—invent" (250). The reference here is to charming and fiery Katya, a little princess in Dostoevsky's own novel *Netochka Nezvanova* (1848–49). At one point, Dostoevsky has four different suggestions to himself, one after another: "NECESSARY: To develop the Idiot's personality masterfully. Stop it at an interesting juncture of the novel. More gravity in the novel. The Idiot's personality" (208). Dostoevsky's novels were published in installments, and he tried to stop each installment at as suspenseful a juncture as possible.

At one point Dostoevsky asks himself: "How to make the hero's person more attractive [*simpatichnee*] to the reader?" He then answers his own question: "If Don Quixote and Pickwick, being virtuous characters, are attractive to the reader and were also successful, this is by virtue of the fact that they are funny. The hero of the novel, the Prince, while he is not funny, has another attractive trait: he is *innocent!*" (239).

Dostoevsky's notebooks show him searching both for a plot and for a cast of characters. His early notebook entries are far removed from what became *The Idiot*. The initial nucleus of the novel was what eventually became the Ivolgin family: the family of a ruined landowner (in later versions he becomes a retired general) trying to make a go of it in St. Petersburg. There are two sons: "the handsome one," who will be Ganya, and "the epileptic," downtrodden, troubled, yet proud and passionate one. A daughter is engaged to an officer who is also a moneylender. She remains and marries Ptitsyn, a moneylender, though not an officer.

In the third plan ("new and *last* plan," a phrase that recurs in the notebooks) another general and his family are introduced, and the parents of the first family have high hopes that "the handsome one" will marry an heiress and improve the family's condition—recognizably Ganya's dream to marry Aglaya. A fourth plan moves the Idiot from "the family" to an "Uncle," who for some time seems to be destined to play a major role in the novel. In subsequent plans the Idiot is jerked back and forth between the "Uncle" and the "General." These plans are dotted with attempts to generate drama, all of which are immediately discarded. Some of the themes developed show up in the novel, others do not. The rivalry of two women, the Idiot's fondness for children, a bride fleeing her wedding, an encounter in a railway carriage, and even the theme of a man offering to burn his finger on a candle to prove his love (in the novel Aglaya asks Ganya for such proof in jest) appear in the novel. The rape of a young girl by the Idiot, the Idiot's illegitimacy, Ganya's strangling Aglaya, and many other motifs, some of them very strange, do not.

The genesis of the character who becomes Nastasya Filippovna is tortuous. Its earliest version is Mignon, an adopted daughter of the "main family," who almost immediately merges with Olga Umetsky, a young girl whose name had recently made headlines in the Russian press. Olga, a victim of parental neglect and abuse, had set fire to the house of her parents. Dostoevsky, to whom child abuse was a lifelong preoccupation, became intensely interested in the case. Mignon is in love with "the handsome one" and hates his fiancee. She is raped, by the Idiot in one version and by "the handsome one" in another, but repulses her stepfather's advances. Even when she has become recognizably Nastasya Filippovna, her fate is far from firmly set. At one point she is married to the Prince. In one entry, she runs off to a brothel. In another, Aglaya becomes passionately attached to her and begs her forgiveness.

The figure of the character who will be Aglaya is hardly more stable. She is "extraordinarily beautiful and haughty" as well as "cutting and mocking." At one point she rejects a senator's hand, although he has "a million and a half," finally accepts "the Uncle's," but on the eve of the wedding "flees with the Idiot." She then returns to "the Uncle," while the Idiot pairs up with Olga Umetsky.

But all these vagaries are nothing compared to the metamorphoses that the Idiot undergoes in Dostoevsky's notebooks. He is from the outset an epileptic, writes a good hand, and is "secretly" in love with Hero, who will later become Aglaya. But he is a man of "strong passions, a burning desire to be loved, and inordinate pride." It is out of pride that "he wants to control and subdue himself" (141). He violates Mignon, who "submits freely, though without love," although she "almost killed the handsome one" when he made tipsy advances to her. The Idiot is projected to change through the power of love and to become compassionate and forgiving. At this early stage the Idiot has a mother who hates him. She is responsible for his reputation as an "idiot." The Idiot's dual nature is a recurrent theme: "Who is he? A terrible villain or a mysterious ideal?" (195).

The first mention of Christ is associated not with the Idiot but with "a most noble figure" identified only as "the Son," who is the Idiot's rival for Hero's love. A little later it develops that the Idiot is the illegitimate son of "the Uncle." Yet a few pages later we find a note that points directly to the definitive version of the novel: "Railway carriage. Getting acquainted. A conversation. They seem to become friends. Meeting the general's family" (163). Following his usual habit, Dostoevsky had anything but a clear picture of the entire plot while installments of his novel were appearing in print. A few pages later the Idiot "was married to a girl with an illegitimate child" who is likened to "Holbein's madonna." She eventually dies, leaving him in "Byronic despair" (190). At this point Dostoevsky seems to be getting close to the definitive version, but then the notes take off again in a wholly different direction, that of Olga Umetsky's defloration and other vagaries.

Very slowly the Idiot acquires the traits that mark him in the definitive text. He becomes a Prince, then a "fool in Christ" (*yurodivyi*), and it is only on 9 April, at a time when Dostoevsky was well into printing his novel, that the entry THE PRINCE CHRIST twice appears on the margin of a page. The same entry is repeated on the following day.

Other characters undergo similar transformations. Ippolit shows up relatively late, on 10 March: "Invent a role in the plot for Ganya, Ippolit, etc. and Varya" (218). An entry on 15 September is significant for the interpretation of the novel as a whole: "IPPOLIT is the main axis of the whole novel. He is out to take possession even of the Prince, yet when it comes right down to it realizes that he can never get control over him" (277). At this time Dostoevsky appears to have wanted to give Ippolit a greater role in the novel, but it was too late to give him a role in the main plot, and Ippolit remained a figure important only on the philosophical plane of the novel.

Rogozhin also shows up late, and his role is not immediately established. At one point Dostoevsky considered letting him develop a liaison with Aglaya. It is conceivable that Rogozhin developed from the dark and violent side of the Idiot's personality as initially conceived.

Evgeny Pavlovich Radomsky is initially called Velmonchek. He is characterized as "a charming personality, with a perennial and constant subtle, mocking and condescending smile." His uncle, who shoots himself after having embezzled a huge sum of government funds, is identified as "Politkovsky." One Aleksei Gavrilovich Politkovsky had committed suicide in 1853. After his death it was discovered that he had embezzled and squandered 1,400,000 rubles of the fund for invalids of which he was in charge. A note related to Velmonchek reads: "*Don Juan.* (Marries Lebedev's daughter—for the strangeness of it, having been rejected by Aglaya, to show off.)" (270). In the epilogue of the definitive version there is a hint that Evgeny Pavlovich may come back and marry Vera Lebedev. In the notebooks, Dostoevsky is still in doubt about his fate; one entry has him kill himself. However, his position versus Prince Myshkin is stated clearly: "Velmonchek continually laughs at the Prince and makes fun of him. A sceptic and unbeliever. He sincerely finds everything about the Prince ridiculous, to the very last moment" (274).

Beyond specific instances in which the notebooks may help in interpreting the definitive text, they give the critical reader insight into a highly sophisticated and conscious craftsman who was much concerned with the form of his work. They reveal a writer who worked with preconceived ideas for which he tried to find an appropriate concrete expression. He was a writer who did not copy from nature but created his characters in his own imagination, unlike writers such as Turgenev, who claimed that he avoided introducing characters in his fiction whom he had not met in real life. There is no indication in the notebooks to *The Idiot* that Dostoevsky consciously identified himself with the Idiot or any direct allusion to his relationship with either Apollinaria Suslova or Anna Korvin-Krukovsky.

5

The Evidence from Dostoevsky's Correspondence

Dostoevsky's correspondence is relevant to a reading of *The Idiot* for several reasons: it contains information regarding the intent governing the writer's work; it offers some hints toward an interpretation of the novel; it also suggests aspects of his work that Dostoevsky was unsure or critical of. Dostoevsky's principal correspondents at the time he was working on *The Idiot* were Nikolai Strakhov, the poet Apollon Maikov (1821–97), an old friend, and his young niece Sofya Aleksandrovna Ivanova (1847–1907).

Dominating Dostoevsky's statements about *The Idiot* is the basic idea that in this novel he will "portray a perfectly good man" and that this will be exceedingly difficult. In a letter of 1 January 1868 to Ivanova he writes:

> So about three weeks ago I started a new novel and began working day and night. The idea of the novel is an old favorite of mine, but it was so difficult that for a long time I wouldn't dare to tackle it, and if I have done so now it was only because I was in a state verging on despair. The

main idea of the novel is to portray a positively good man. There is nothing more difficult in the world, and this is particularly true today. All writers, not only ours but Europeans as well, who have attempted to portray the *positively* good have always given up, because the problem is a boundless one. Perfection is an ideal, and this ideal, whether it be ours or civilized Europe's, is still far from a realization. There is only one positively good figure in the world, namely Christ, so that the appearance of that infinitely good figure is in itself a miracle. (The entire Gospel after St. John is a statement to this effect; he finds the whole miracle in the Incarnation alone, in the manifestation of the Good alone.)

However, I am anticipating too much. I shall mention only that, of the positive figures in Christian literature, the most perfect is that of Don Quixote. But he is good only because he is also ridiculous. The figure of Dickens' Pickwick (a conception infinitely weaker than that of Don Quixote, but still a tremendous one) is also ridiculous, and that is the only reason why it is successful. Compassion for a good man who is ridiculed and who is unaware of his own worth creates sympathy in the reader. And this ability to arouse compassion is the very secret of humor. Jean Valjean is another powerful effort, but he engenders sympathy because of his terrible misfortune and society's injustice to him. But there is nothing of this sort in my novel, absolutely nothing, and this is why I am terribly afraid that it will be a positive failure.[10]

Dostoevsky said much the same in a letter to Maikov written a day earlier. He complained that his hero was "still extremely pale," even though he was "not so vague" in his heart (*PSS,* 28:241).

The passage in Dostoevsky's letter to Ivanova in which he brings up the Gospel after St. John testifies to the writer's Johannine orientation, confirmed by Dostoevsky's markings in his New Testament, which is extant. A Johannine emphasis on religion as God's word made incarnate is a key feature of Orthodox Christendom and of Dostoevsky's Christian sensibility. The letter is also important in that it stresses the importance of *Don Quixote* for Dostoevsky's conception of his hero.

Time and again Dostoevsky complains in his letters about the difficulties he has with his hero and worries about whether he will succeed in realizing his idea. On 30 March 1868 he writes to his niece: "The idea of the novel is one whose strength lies not in its immediate effect, but in its very essence. That essence is beautiful in its original concept, but how will it come off when written down?" (*PSS*, 28:292). This and similar statements suggest that the intended meaning of the novel is not explicit or specifically stated but has to be grasped from the text as a whole.

Another recurrent complaint is that he must work hurriedly and therefore may spoil his work. On 26 October 1868—that is, quite close to the completion of his novel—Dostoevsky writes to Maikov: "And then, Part 4 (it is long—12 sheets) is the crucial one, and all my hopes rest with it! Now that everything has become crystal clear, I have come to the bitter conclusion that never before in my career as a writer have I had a better and richer poetic idea than the one that has taken shape in a detailed plan which I have worked out for Part 4. But so what? I must rush ahead at full speed, write without rereading, hurry like mad and, in the end, still miss my deadline!" (*PSS*, 28:321).

A letter written to Ivanova on the same day has been seen by some as the key to the structure of the whole novel: "Finally, the main thing is for me that my fourth part and its conclusion are the most important thing in my novel, that is, it is almost so that the whole novel was in fact written and invented for the sake of the denouement" (*PSS*, 28:313). This remark has been interpreted to the effect that Dostoevsky literally conceived the finale before he worked out the details of the plot leading up to it. The notebooks suggest that this was not the case. A note dated 4 October reads: "Rogozhin and the Prince by the corpse. *Final. Not bad*" (283). This suggests that this idea had just occurred to Dostoevsky and that he liked it. Most of the novel was completed by then.

A significant point that emerges with great clarity from Dostoevsky's correspondence is that he realizes that his novel, and in particular its main character, are "fantastic," but also that he believes that his fantastic view of the world is closer to reality than the view conveyed by his realist rivals Turgenev, Pisemsky, Goncharov, and so on. In a letter to Maikov dated 11 December 1868 he writes: "I have a wholly different conception of reality and realism than our realists and critics" (*PSS,* 28:329). He goes on to say that his idealism is more real than their realism and points to the fantastic developments in Russian society in the preceding years as evidence of his contention. The utmost that realism has accomplished along the lines of creating a "positively beautiful man," he says, is Aleksandr Ostrovsky's Lyubim Tortsov. That, he says, is as far as realism will venture in presenting an ideal. (Lyubim Tortsov in Ostrovsky's play *Poverty Is No Vice* is the drunken and destitute brother of a rich merchant who has squandered his patrimony but retained a heart and conscience.)

In a letter to Strakhov of 26 February 1869, after having read some of the negative reviews of his novel, Dostoevsky writes:

> I have my own peculiar view of reality (in art), and that which a majority [of critics and writers] calls almost fantastic and exceptional, sometimes contains for me the very essence of reality. A [presentation of] a number of ordinary day-to-day phenomena and a routine view of these is not, in my opinion, enough to make for realism, but rather the contrary. . . . Is not my fantastic *Idiot* reality, and most ordinary day-to-day reality at that? It is precisely now that such characters [must appear] in those strata of our society that are torn away from the soil, strata that become fantastic in reality. But *no use* talking! Much in the novel is written hurriedly, much is longwinded and didn't come off right,

but some things did. I am not defending my novel, but I will
stand behind my idea. (*PSS*, 29:19)

Here one *pochvennik* addresses another. The *pochvenniki* believed that whole segments of Russia's educated classes had become so alienated from the vital traditions and concerns of the
Russian people that they no longer stood on firm ground but
rather floated in the thin air of their theoretical ratiocinations.
This letter suggests that in *The Idiot* Dostoevsky already had in
mind what he would make quite explicit in his next novel, *The
Possessed*—namely, that in his opinion Russian life had reached
a stage that could be called fantastic, removed from common-
sense reality, and inexplicable in conventional rational terms.

6

Personal Elements in

The Idiot

To a reader familiar with Dostoevsky's biography, some details and patterns of *The Idiot* may appear as projections of the writer's personal experience. Dostoevsky's novels, however, with the exception of *Notes from the House of the Dead,* have generally a limited personal subtext. *The Idiot* has more of it than any of the other great novels. The descriptions of Myshkin's epileptic fits are based on Dostoevsky's personal experience, as are Myshkin's observations on the mental state of a condemned man, at least to some extent. (Elements from Victor Hugo's *The Last Day of a Condemned Man* also appear to have entered these pages.)

The Prince's relations with the Epanchin family in the setting of a summer in Pavlovsk, and possibly his vacillating between Aglaya and Nastasya Filippovna, too, may very well reflect Dostoevsky's own experience. In 1865, when he courted Anna Vasilyevna Korvin-Krukovsky, who had published two stories in *Epokha,* his stormy relationship with Apollinaria Suslova was anything but forgotten. Anna's mother, Elizaveta Fyodorovna, née Schubert, appears to have resembled Mme

Epanchina of *The Idiot*, and her relationship with Dostoevsky was also similar to that of Mme Epanchina and Prince Myshkin, though she was only a year older than her daughter's suitor. The Korvin-Krukovskys had a dacha in Pavlovsk, and Dostoevsky often visited there. The head of the family was, like Ivan Fyodorovich Epanchin, a general.

As was common in nineteenth-century novels, the author's own opinions were often put into the mouth of his characters. In *The Idiot*—but not necessarily in Dostoevsky's other novels—the narrator's opinions generally are the author's. But it is also Dostoevsky's practice to have his views expressed by various characters, not only attractive, positive, and reliable characters but also despicable and unreliable ones. Much of what Myshkin says in the course of the novel was, of course, in accord with Dostoevsky's own views. But the same is true of many of the things said by Evgeny Pavlovich Radomsky or even by the fraud and liar Lebedev. Myshkin's views on the death penalty, on the Catholic church, on Russian extremism and Russian messianism were certainly Dostoevsky's. We know from Anna Grigoryevna's memoirs that Myshkin's reaction to Holbein's *Deposition of Christ* ("Why, that picture might make some people lose their faith" [250/182]) was her husband's own. But Evgeny Pavlovich's views on Russian liberals and the lack of originality in Russian thought and literature were also Dostoevsky's, and so were Lebedev's ideas, however grotesquely expressed, that modern society lacked "any idea binding mankind together with anything like the power it had in those [earlier] centuries" (420/315) and that "the law of self-destruction and the law of self-preservation are equally strong in humanity!" (415/311). When Lebedev says that the Lord will perhaps forgive the Countess Du Barry for that *encore un moment* because a human soul cannot go any further in misery (228/164), he may be conveying to the reader Dostoevsky's own view of Nastasya Filippovna.

Suggestions have been made regarding specific prototypes

of Nastasya Filippovna and Rogozhin. As to the former, the character of Apollinaria Suslova seems more relevant to the novel than any superficial coincidence of family circumstances discovered by scholars in Dostoevsky's extended family. Suslova was an extraordinarily beautiful woman, and her diaries show her to be as proud and headstrong as Nastasya Filippovna and equally inclined to irrational self-laceration. As to Rogozhin, the story of a stern tightwad father and his spendthrift son happened over and over again around Dostoevsky. However, the detail of keeping a body in one's house surrounded by vessels with a disinfectant-deodorant was taken from a criminal case reported by the *Moscow News* on 29 November 1867. The murderer was a Moscow merchant of good family; like Rogozhin he was sentenced to fifteen years at hard labor.

The several other murders discussed in the novel, including the one where the murderer begs God's forgiveness as he stabs his victim, were all taken from the contemporary Russian press. However, Dostoevsky slanted the motives and circumstances of these crimes to fit his moral and religious message. The man who murdered his friend for his silver watch needed the money to go home to his family. The circumstances of two separate murders committed by two highly intelligent students, Danilov and Gorsky, were more complex than Lebedev (224/161) or Evgeny Pavlovich (376/279) see them in the novel.

A number of specific details of the novel may be linked to Dostoevsky's personal life. Myshkin is the son of an impoverished nobleman and a Moscow woman of the merchant class, the same as Dostoevsky himself. Myshkin writes a beautiful hand, and so did Dostoevsky. Myshkin has stayed in Switzerland for a long time, and so did Dostoevsky. The story of the drunken soldier who sells his tin cross to Myshkin, claiming that it is silver (252/183), happened to Dostoevsky himself, according to his wife, who also reported that her husband had told her of his frequent dreams of a battle in which the Austrians, of all people, were routed—Myshkin, in conversation with

Aglaya (489/354) also imagines himself defeating the Austrians. When Lebedev spins his yarn about having lost a leg in battle and replaced it with a "Chernosvitov leg" (544/411), this is not only another occurrence of a motif ("lameness or loss of a leg") that accompanies Dostoevsky through much of his career, but also a personal reminiscence. Rafail Aleksandrovich Chernosvitov, the inventor of a prosthetic limb, was a member of the Petrashevsky circle whom Dostoevsky had known in the late 1840s. Such instances of personal subtext may be easily multiplied.

7

The Literary Subtext

The Idiot, like other novels by Dostoevsky, has an extensive and varied literary subtext. Many literary quotes from and allusions to a variety of works of Russian and Western literatures can be found throughout the text, simply reflecting the literary culture of the day: Dostoevsky was addressing a literate reader who would recognize a quote from Shakespeare, Voltaire, Goethe, Pushkin, or Lermontov. Other more significant quotes and allusions advance the plot or the argument of the novel.

Only a few examples of the first category may be presented here. When the clown Ferdyshchenko is made to quote the first two lines of a fable by Ivan Krylov (166/117), it is assumed that the reader knows its last line—"All's easier than to suffer indignities from an ass"—which means that the joke is on the dignified Totsky. When it is said that Keller used to stop passersby on Nevsky Prospect "begging assistance in the language of Marlinsky" (186/133), it is understood that the reader remembers the florid romantic style of Aleksandr Bestuzhev-Marlinsky (1797–1837). When Ippolit quotes from memory,

"The sun resounded in the sky," and asks, "Who wrote that line?," the reader is expected to recognize this as a line from the prologue to Goethe's *Faust*. *La dame aux camélias* by Dumas *fils* is mentioned explicitly (179/128), and camelias are the leitmotiv of Totsky's anecdote told at Nastasya Filippovna's name-day party. The implied point is that Totsky would like her to play the role of Marguerite Gautier and that she refuses to oblige. By the way, Ferdyshchenko's anecdote on the same occasion is stolen from Rousseau's *Confessions*.

Myshkin's observations on life in prison (82/51) clearly echo Byron's "The Prisoner of Chillon," which in Zhukovsky's translation was very popular in Russia. In the wedding scene (648/492) a clerk, overwhelmed by Nastasya Filippovna's beauty, yells: "A princess! For such a princess I would sell my soul. 'At the price of your life, a night with me!'" This is a quote from Pushkin's "Egyptian Nights" and the words are Cleopatra's. This is cruelly ironic, since it is Nastasya Filippovna who will die before the sun rises again and not her lover as in Pushkin's poem. Shortly before her death, too, Nastasya Filippovna has been reading Flaubert's *Madame Bovary* (656/499). Myshkin finds the book on her table as he is looking for her after their aborted wedding. It can be understood as a subtle signal that he is looking for a dead woman.

There are instances in which a quote or an allusion is more explicitly inserted to score a point. The ditty "Dear little Lyov for five long years" (300/221) is a parodic response to a nasty personal attack on Dostoevsky by Mikhail Saltykov-Shchedrin, whose jingle "Fedya did not pray to God" was published in the satirical journal *The Whistle* (no. 9, 1863). Calling Malthus "that friend of humanity" (416/312) is an ironic jibe not only at Malthus but at contemporary social Darwinism as well. General Ivolgin's reminiscences about Napoleon in Moscow in 1812 (543/415–16) are a dig at the numerous self-glorifying memoirs that kept appearing in Russia even as the memory of that glorious year was fading. The phrase "contemporary nihilism revealed by Mr. Turgenev" (627/476) is an ironic jibe at the liberal Turgenev in that it ludicrously overstates the importance of his novel *Fathers and Sons* (1862), whose hero is the nihilist Bazarov. Other such instances of a polemic subtext could be singled out.

In some instances a literary quotation is used to illustrate a point related to the narrator's views on the art of fiction. For example, Gogol's Podkolyosin from the comedy *Marriage*, Pirogov from the short story "Nevsky Prospect," as well as Molière's George Dandin from the comedy of that title come up in connection with various observations concerning literary types (507–09/383–85).

Even more important are those instances in which a literary quotation or allusion becomes an integral element of the novel's plot or of its philosophic argument. The emphatic mention of *Don Quixote* (219/157), and particularly in conjunction with Pushkin's ballad "The Poor Knight" (285/209), establishes Prince Myshkin's kinship with the knight of the sad countenance. (Dostoevsky's notebooks and letters corroborate this connection.) The reading by Aglaya of the ballad about the knight who fell in love with the Virgin and died "silent, sad, bereft of reason" (286/209), with the initials *AMD* (*Ave, Mater Dei*) replaced by *NFB* (Nastasya Filippovna Barashkova), advances the plot of the novel as it reveals that Aglaya is jealous of Nastasya Filippovna and foreshadows Myshkin's fate.

The quatrain from Nicolas-Joseph Gilbert's "Adieux," falsely attributed to Millevoye (456/343), is quoted to be bitterly attacked as maudlin hypocrisy. Yet it does in fact stand for Myshkin's attitude, even though he can deeply empathize with Ippolit's ironic putdown. A passage just preceding the quote from Gilbert deplores the inability of man to join in the harmony of nature and "share in the banquet and the chorus" (455/343). It is repeated by Myshkin a few pages later (466/352). This passage is an echo of a poem by Fyodor Tyutchev (1803–73), whose last stanza reads

Hence and how did this dissonance arise?
And why is it that in this common chorus
The soul does not chant what the sea does,
And why does the thinking reed murmur?
("There Is Melody in the Waves of the Sea," 1865)

Both Dostoevsky's passage and Tyutchev's poem echo the platonic notion of man's lost harmony with the rhythm of the cosmos.

By far the most important literary subtext of *The Idiot* is the biblical. It has two foci—Christ's death on the cross and the Apocalypse. When Myshkin says, "It is of this agony and this torture that Christ spoke, too" (44/21), he alludes to Matthew, chapter 26, verses 38–39 (Christ in Gethsemane), and when Ippolit gets to the subject of the Crucifixion (451/339) he refers directly to Mark, chapter 5, verse 41, and Matthew, chapter 27, verse 32. Ippolit, by the way, is credited with quite extraordinary theological sophistication, as he is made to say, "I know that the Christian Church laid it down, even in the early ages, that Christ's suffering was not symbolical but actual, and that His body was therefore fully and completely subject to the laws of nature on the cross" (450/339). Here Ippolit rejects the so-called Apollinarian heresy, a key point in Russian Orthodox doctrine. Russian churchmen have often claimed that the Western church fell into and persisted in that heresy.

The Revelation of John the Divine appears explicitly in connection with Lebedev's mostly ludicrous applications of the apocalyptic text to contemporary Russia, such as when the network of railroads covering Russia is identified with "the star called Wormwood" of Revelation, chapter 8, verses 10–11 (341/254). However, as so often in Dostoevsky, the grotesque and ridiculous provides, as it were, a backdoor entrance to a serious idea, in this case, to the idea that Russia has indeed reached a crucial point in its history. Significantly, Ippolit also explicitly quotes the Apocalypse ("that there should be time no longer" [Revelation 10:6]) just before reading his "Essential Explanation" (425/318). Some critics have suggested that the "Essential Explanation" itself contains subliminal allusions to the Apocalypse.

Regrettably, much of the literary and even of the biblical subtext is lost on the contemporary reader, particularly in translation.

8

Composition

Several critics have noted that *The Idiot* may be read and interpreted on more than one level of understanding. Konstantin Mochulsky, in his important study *Dostoevsky: His Life and Work,* sees a dual structure in the novel—one empirical, the other metaphysical.[11] Mochulsky's definition of the metaphysical plane, however, although not unfounded, seems to stretch the textual evidence too far. Although Lebedev, a character who in his own grotesque fashion says some thoughtful things, does apply the Apocalypse to contemporary Russia, there is little in the novel to suggest that Lebedev's "interpretation" of the Apocalypse is to be taken seriously, much less to be applied to *The Idiot* as a whole. Harold Rosenberg, in the splendid essay "*The Idiot:* Second Century," plausibly suggests that a tragic drama is inserted into "the vast disorder of episodes . . . and the activities of subordinate and late-appearing characters—such as Ippolit—that constitute the real body of the novel."[12] Skaftymov, in his study "The Thematic Composition of *The Idiot,*" suggests that "an inner thematic meaning undoubtedly dominates over the whole structure of the novel," calling this its "teleological principle."[13] Skaftymov makes a good case for this conception, though he is somewhat selective in choosing the material that he finds structurally relevant.

The levels of meaning extracted from the text depend on the reader's understanding of them. For instance, the literary subtext of *The Idiot* (discussed in chapter 7) is accessible only to a reader who is familiar with the works alluded to by Dostoevsky. In this chapter several different levels of meaning are suggested to the reader, with the understanding that the reader has the privilege to accept or reject them.

On a literal level, requiring no special knowledge or erudition, *The Idiot* is a rather typical nineteenth-century novel featuring much psychological analysis, some social commentary, many journalistic and essayistic digressions, and a wealth of literary quotes and allusions that the reader may or may not recognize as such. On a moral and religious level, *The Idiot* deals with some basic questions of ethics and metaphysics, explicitly as well as implicitly. The explicit discussion of the death penalty early in the novel, seemingly an essayistic digression, is in fact part of a discourse on the antinomy of the presence of death in God's world that is carried on throughout the novel. On a moral level, the insertion of Marie's story in chapter 6 of part 1 is meaningful as an implicit comment on the heroine, Nastasya Filippovna.

An allegoric reading of *The Idiot* resting on the recognition of Prince Myshkin as a Christ figure is supported by many intrinsic details as well as by information gathered from Dostoevsky's notebooks. A psychoanalytic reading of *The Idiot* has been attempted. If its premises are accepted, the plot of the novel acquires a wholly different dimension, as does the author's relationship to his work. Finally, a mystic undercurrent may be detected, particularly by a reader inclined to read *The Idiot* as a Christian novel, that is, as the presentation of a world in which God's presence is felt and God's law is intact, a theodicy in the sense that *The Brothers Karamazov* is one.

The Idiot is, at least on the surface, structured like many nineteenth-century novels from Russia as well as the West. The drift of its narrative lacks the powerful undertow that gives *Crime and Punishment* its extraordinary dramatic tension. The narrator often stops or diverts the flow of the narrative. He does so in several different ways. Information is withheld from the reader. There are gaps in the Prince's past. We are not told where and how he acquired an education (he is obviously a well-educated man) or his paleographic and calligraphic skills. The reader does not learn about Myshkin's inheritance until the end of part 1, nearly two hundred pages into the novel. Later, the reader is left in the dark about events between the end of part 1 and the beginning of part 2. There are some other minor gaps.

The train of events is repeatedly abandoned for various digressions, some of them quite lengthy, such as the inserted novellas, the life of Marie as told by Prince Myshkin, and Ippolit's "Essential Explanation." Various anecdotes are told by Prince Myshkin, General Ivolgin, and Lebedev, as well as by those attending Nastasya Filippovna's nameday party. References are made to several notorious criminal cases.

The text contains scraps of information and discussions on a variety of topics, some of which are relevant to the novel's main theme. For instance, the Prince's lengthy discourse on the death penalty is relevant to what may be the novel's central theme, as are the several accounts of executions introduced in the course of the novel. But the narrator's essay at the beginning of part 3 on Russian inefficiency due to a tendency to follow the crowd and refuse to take the initiative is hardly relevant to any major theme of the novel. The same may be said of the narrator's essays on literary types who in real life appear in watered down versions (507–08/383–84), on the absence of practical men in Russia (363–65/268–70), and so on. Prince Myshkin's long diatribe in which he airs Dostoevsky's anti-Catholic and Slavophile ideas (594–97/450–53) clearly serves an end beyond that of advancing the plot. Altogether, *The Idiot* has more of a journalistic component than other novels by Dostoevsky. Its text is a catchall for a variety of opinions, polemic sorties, worldly wisdom, character sketches, and witticisms.

It must be noted that these digressions were not held against Dostoevsky as artistically inappropriate by his readers or even by his critics. The novel was then still considered an open form that allowed the introduction of almost any amount of interesting feuilletonistic material, often triggered by recent events of topical interest. Rogozhin's vigil over Nastasya Filippovna's body with several open bottles of disinfectant around her bed would be recognized by contemporary readers as a detail of a recent sensational murder case. Similar examples are readily adduced from Dostoevsky's other novels, as well as from the novels of his contemporaries—Tolstoi's *Anna Karenina,* for example.

The Idiot is inconsistent in the foregrounding of its main characters. Prince Myshkin appears throughout the text, but Ippolit, who at least on one level of the novel is Myshkin's main antagonist, has a minor role until he takes center stage to deliver his "Essential Explanation," only to fade away into the background thereafter. The heroine, Nastasya Filippovna, has several dramatic scenes but disappears from the stage for long stretches of the narrative.

Although *The Idiot* invites a reading on several levels of understanding, it is also, at least among Dostoevsky's major works, closer in most respects to an ordinary nineteenth-century novel. Judging by his notebooks Dostoevsky appears to have contemplated a family setting. In the original plan the rather Dickensian Ivolgin family was central to the plot, but it was pushed back to the fringes of the action in the actual text. The nuptial frustrations of General Epanchin's nubile daughters could be part of a novel by, say, Jane Austen. The breakfast of the Epanchin women early in part 1 would serve as an excellent introduction to a family novel. The romance of Aglaya and Prince Myshkin, at least initially, develops in a way that fits the model of a conventional nineteenth-century love story. Aglaya is a not unfamiliar novelistic character. A beautiful, headstrong, proud, intelligent, but virginally naive young lady, she falls in love with Prince Myshkin at first sight. True to the nature of her character, she will not admit her enamoration, not even to herself. The Prince, equally innocent, only slowly realizes that he reciprocates her feelings. But a happy ending does not appear impossible. Subsequently the reader witnesses several scenes with the Epanchin family, and a number of details in a lighter vein are presented that would seem to suggest a love story with a happy ending rather than a hideous tragedy: the Prince assumes that Aglaya's reading of Pushkin's ballad with *NFB* substituted for *AMD* (285/209) is a mere "childish prank," but of course it tells the reader that she is in love with Myshkin and jealous of Nastasya Filippovna. In a scene at the Epanchins' home Aglaya literally declares her love, then snaps at her mother for saying that she is in love, and finally breaks out into merry laughter when the Prince, confused and terrified, responds that he had never thought of asking for her hand (381–83/283–84). There is a comic intimation that haughty, rebellious Aglaya may not know all the facts about sex (473–74/358). Finally, there is the merry episode with the hedgehog (559–60/423–24), quite close to the final catastrophe.

The other Epanchins are all the type of characters one knows from comedy and from love novels in a lighter vein. Lizaveta Prokofyevna, lively and warmhearted, is also a comic character. The character sketch of her (365–70/270–74), an exercise in humorous ambiguity, also makes good sense psychologically. Her husband is likewise the butt of the narrator's irony yet also a realistically drawn character. Aglaya's sisters play their supporting roles in a conventional way.

Of course, the reader's expectations for an ordinary love novel are frustrated. Late in the novel Lizaveta Prokofyevna exclaims, "Aglaya Ivanovna loved like a woman, like a human being, and not like an abstract spirit" (637/484). What had started and developed as a conventional love novel turns into a tragedy within whose plan Aglaya, a nontragic character, becomes irrelevant.

The Ivolgin family also is well suited to appear in a nineteenth-century family novel. The tragicomic and Dickensian figure of General Ivolgin, irrelevant to the main plot, provides some early comic relief and some profuse tear jerking in the end. The other Ivolgins are exercises in the ordinary. "Nature loves such people and is kind to them" (512/387), the narrator says of Ptitsyn, General Ivolgin's son-in-law. Ganya Ivolgin occasions the narrator's disquisition on ordinary people in chapter 1 of part 4. As the novel moved away from the model of the family novel and toward that of tragedy, Ganya, too, was displaced to the fringes of the plot.

Altogether, then, *The Idiot* contains many elements of a realist family novel, but these elements merely serve as background to the tragedy of the three protagonists, Prince Myshkin, Nastasya Filippovna, and Rogozhin.

The Idiot paints a fairly broad panoramic picture of St. Petersburg in the late 1860s—that is, a period of rapid social and economic change marked by the emergence of a modern capitalist economy, a broad spectrum of political philosophies, and highly volatile and often internecine journalism. Money plays as great a role in the plot of *The Idiot* as it does in any novel by Balzac. Every character is affected by money in some way, and many specific amounts of money, large and small, figure in the plot. Ganya is to marry Nastasya Filippovna for a dowry of 75,000 rubles. Rogozhin's infatuation with her is reflected in a series of financial transactions, starting with his cashing of two 5,000-ruble bonds. Heir to his father's millions, Rogozhin offers to buy Nastasya Filippovna for 100,000 rubles. Prince Myshkin is expected to inherit over a million but at last report has 135,000 rubles in cash. Myshkin has sent Burdovsky 250 rubles and offers him 10,000. Lebedev pleads a case in small claims court. If he wins, he will get fifty rubles; if he loses, five. General Ivolgin steals 400 rubles from Lebedev. This list could be extended. Some characters—Totsky, General Epanchin, Rogozhin—are involved with big money. Others—the moneylenders Ptitsyn and Lebedev—move money on a modest scale. Keller, Burdovsky and his friends try to scrounge a few rubles. Money is the cause of scandal and crime on every level of society. Evgeny Pavlovich's uncle, a high dignitary, shoots himself after having embezzled 350,000 rubles government money. General Ivolgin becomes a thief. Several recent murder and robbery stories are favored conversation topics.

The whole political spectrum, from the conservative Right to the nihilist Left, is represented among the characters of the novel. A great deal of ideological talk is presented. Lebedev's nephew and his friends spout the rhetoric of the radical Left (298–300/217–19). Readers hear a spirited spontaneous reaction to the nihilist ethos from Mme Epanchin (320/237–38) and acidly sarcastic criticism of the radical as well as the liberal positions from the aristocratic Evgeny Pavlovich (part 2, chapters 9 and 10; part 3, chapter 1). Dostoevsky's antiradical and antiliberal bias is evident. The generous and warmhearted Lizaveta Prokofyevna and the intelligent and well-educated Evgeny Pavlovich express Dostoevsky's own views. The radicals are represented by a bunch of unsavory or callow young men. Their ideological positions are presented as rhetoric absurdly at variance with the facts. When it has turned out that young Burdovsky has no legitimate claim to Myshkin's money after all, he returns 100 of the 250 rubles he had received from him. Lebedev's nephew, speaking for the group, explains:

> Of course a hundred roubles is not two hundred and fifty, and it's not just the same, but the principle is what matters. The initiative is the great thing, and that a hundred and fifty roubles are missing is only a detail. What matters is, that Burdovsky does not accept your charity, your excellency, that he throws it in your face, and in that sense it makes no

difference whether it's a hundred or two hundred and fifty (317/236).

Dostoevsky's point—a point he would make repeatedly in both his fiction and his journalism—is that the ideas and principles of progressives were pure theory and wholly unrelated to any real facts of Russian life—or to their own practices.

Mme Epanchin says, "They don't believe in God, they don't believe in Christ! Why, you are so eaten up with pride and vanity that you'll end by eating up one another, that's what I prophesy" (320–21/238). This was precisely Dostoevsky's own opinion. The same is true of Evgeny Pavlovich's assertion that liberals elsewhere may be opposed to the existing order of things and would like to correct it but Russian liberals attack Russia herself: "My liberal has reached a point where he rejects Russia herself, that is, he hates and beats his mother" (374/277). Dostoevsky was going to develop these positions, along with much further accusatory material, in his next novel, *The Possessed*. Returning to an argument he had first developed in *Crime and Punishment*, Dostoevsky lets Evgeny Pavlovich bring up the point that a liberal lawyer of the new generation would feel justified in defending a murderer on the grounds that "considering the poverty of the criminal, it must have been *natural* for him to think of murdering these six people" (376/279) and then lets Myshkin retort that in the past, criminals, though perhaps unrepentant, still knew that they had committed a crime, while the modern criminal believes that his actions are right (377/280).

In attacking Russian nihilism, Dostoevsky used the occasion to settle some personal accounts. The "satirical" ditty composed by Keller for his article in support of Burdovsky's quest for a share of Myshkin's inheritance is an antiparody of a jingle directed against Dostoevsky a few years earlier by his perennial enemy Mikhail Saltykov-Shchedrin, a leader of the radicals and a pillar of their organs, the *Contemporary* and the *National Annals*. The jingle read as follows:

Composition

Fedya did not pray to God,
"It will be alright even without it!"
He temporized and temporized,
And finally found himself in a jam!
At one time he carefreely
Played with Gogol's *Overcoat*
And passed his time
With the usual foolishness.

The jingle was entitled "Self-Assured Fedya" and alluded to Dostoevsky's misfortune, the suppression of his journal *Time* (in Russian, *Vremya*). Dostoevsky had played with Gogol's story *The Overcoat* in his first novel, *Poor Folk,* which was in a way a *parodie sérieuse* of Gogol's work. Dostoevsky identifies the subject of his parody by bringing it up in connection with certain "provincial sketches" (300/221). Saltykov-Shchedrin was the author of a book entitled *Provincial Sketches*.

Dostoevsky's satire does not stop at exposing the brainless absurdity of the nihilist ideology. Emerging capitalism is treated no more kindly. General Epanchin, a captain of commerce and industry, is presented as an inane and at times ludicrous person. The millionaire Rogozhin is presented in a bilious caricature. Lesser capitalists such as Lebedev look even worse. To cover the whole range from Left to Right, Dostoevsky creates an occasion to put down the conservative Right also. At the Epanchins' party in chapter 7 of part 4 the representatives of conservative aristocratic Russia are presented as shallow, vacuous, and clearly without any hope of a future. Dostoevsky's satire here is mordant, perhaps even more bitter than that directed against the young nihilists.

The woman question (*zhenskii vopros*), high on the agenda of Russian progressives in the 1860s, is not made an issue explicitly in *The Idiot*. It is, however, implicit in Nastasya Filippovna's plight and surfaces repeatedly in the novel. Aglaya has some nihilist ideas. She almost cut off her beautiful hair at one time (367/271): nihilist women wore their hair short, nihilist men wore theirs long, and both wore dark glasses. She dreams of some independent activity outside marriage. Aglaya's clash with Nastasya Filippovna brings the issue to the fore. When Aglaya tries her utmost to insult her rival, she says, "If you'd wanted to be respectable, you'd have become a washerwoman" (623/473). The implication of the whole acrimonious exchange is that an educated woman has no choice but to be a man's kept woman as a wife or mistress or do the most menial work. A feminist reading of *The Idiot* offers rich possibilities.[14]

The Idiot has more, and more interesting, female characters than Dostoevsky's other novels. It also shows a vivid interest in feminine psychology. The narrator does not venture to read the consciousness of Nastasya Filippovna, though he lets Prince Myshkin do it. But he does enter Aglaya's thoughts on occasion (470–71/355–56) and lets her pour out all that is on her mind. He allows the reader to follow Lizaveta Prokofyevna's thoughts in a stream-of-consciousness type manner (556–60/421–24). The battle of the sexes is certainly a major theme in *The Idiot*. Rogozhin's description of his cohabitation with Nastasya Filippovna (240–47/174–79) provides a drastic example, the encounters between Aglaya and Prince Myshkin a milder yet still explicit one.

Like other nineteenth-century novels, especially serial novels, *The Idiot* has multiple plots, though a distinct master plot. The latter revolves around the love quadrangle of Prince Myshkin, Aglaya, Nastasya Filippovna, and Rogozhin. The story of the Ivolgin family is linked to the main plot by fairly tenuous ties. Therefore, whenever the focus of the narrative shifts to General Ivolgin, especially late in part 3, and again in part 4, the progress of the main plot stops. This is particularly noticeable at the juncture of chapters 4 and 5 of part 4: after the general's stroke, the narrator has to double back to events that preceded it. Narrative time devoted to Lebedev and his family is even more marginal to the progress of the main plot. However, both the Ivolgins and the Lebedevs play significant roles on levels other than that of the action of the novel.

Composition

From a viewpoint of action, the introduction of Ippolit and his lengthy "Essential Explanation" (much too long to have actually been read within the time span allotted it in the time schedule of the night in question) is a major digression. It is of course of supreme importance on another level of perception.

There is a six-month gap between the fast and furious action of part 1 and its resumption in part 2. The transition from part 1 to part 2 is brief and perfunctory. The reader learns from it that only two days after his arrival in St. Petersburg Prince Myshkin left for Moscow to receive his legacy, and also that Rogozhin, his band of hangers-on, and Nastasya Filippovna soon went to Moscow. As to what happened there, the narrator purports to know only through hearsay and rumor, and it is little at that. More may be gathered about the movements of the Prince, Nastasya Filippovna, and Rogozhin from scattered references to events that took place between that fateful day in November and Prince Myshkin's return to St. Petersburg in the first days of June. It is left to the reader's attention, memory, and imagination to reconstruct these events. A careful reader will come up with the following.

In Moscow Prince Myshkin took care of his business affairs, settling all too generously with his creditors. He met General Epanchin there on a few occasions. He presented himself to Princess Belokonskaya, Mme Epanchin's elderly relative and patroness, who liked him and introduced him to some "good Moscow homes." In Moscow the relationship of Rogozhin and Nastasya Filippovna went through some hectic peripeties. Twice they were about to get married, and twice Nastasya Filippovna ran off at the last moment. On the second of these occasions she joined Myshkin in an unnamed provincial town, where they lived together for a month, though certainly not as man and wife. In March Nastasya Filippovna left Myshkin, too, apparently with a local landowner, whom she also "fooled," as Rogozhin later tells the Prince.[15] In May she and Rogozhin separately returned to Petersburg. Prior to the beginning of part 2,

Myshkin was in touch with the Ivolgins and perhaps with Le-bedev, too, and wrote a brief note to Aglaya. In May Nastasya Filippovna also wrote several letters to Aglaya.

Although a hiatus in the development of a plot is common enough in nineteenth-century novels, it is atypical of Dostoev-sky, most of whose novels feature continuous action over a pe-riod of a few days or weeks. (Flashbacks, however—sometimes quite lengthy, such as the Prince's story of Marie—are found in all of Dostoevsky's major novels.) The gap between parts 1 and 2 in *The Idiot* may be explained in two ways. It may be simply a flaw, caused by the fact that Dostoevsky, evidently at a loss how to continue his novel after the climactic scene concluding part 1 and severely pressed for time, failed to work out a proper transition to part 2. But the gap may be seen as well motivated, too. The three principals have changed perceptibly as they reap-pear on the scene, and a six-month period of intensely taxing experiences accounts for that. The Prince's obvious familiarity with contemporary Russia seems more plausible after a six-month stay during which he met people from various walks of life. Also, the development and resolution of the plot, as devel-oped in parts 2 to 4, demanded a summer setting.

Nevertheless, the plot of *The Idiot* is flawed by virtue of its asymmetry. The drama of *The Idiot,* after a superb first act, is slow to get moving again, after leaving what should have been the second act largely to the reader's imagination. Parts 2 and 3 show little decisive action to advance the plot. What action there is appears tentative, groping for a convincing resolution. But in part 4 the drama gathers momentum, producing what might be called magnificent acts 4 and 5. Dostoevsky's dramatic style, which tends toward presenting scenes rather than a con-tinuous narrative, causes some of his other novels to have sim-ilar lacunae.

If *The Idiot* is a "tragedy of beauty," as Walter Nigg and others have put it, Nastasya Filippovna rather than Prince Myshkin is the pivot of the novel's structure. Nastasya Filippovna's divine beauty marks her for tragedy. The drama of the novel is then that of the tragic destruction of beauty personified. The men and women around Nastasya Filippovna contribute to her destruction. Beauty is Nastasya Filippovna's leitmotiv. It is developed symphonically, in different tonalities and varying volume. Nastasya Filippovna is introduced offstage in the very first chapter, then her portrait is shown in chapter 3, and in chapter 8 she finally appears in person. After her nameday party, which she dominates, she makes a number of appearances, mostly brief. Each appearance is accompanied by her leitmotiv—her beauty. The plot of the novel, from this viewpoint, takes the form of a vortex that carries Nastasya Filippovna down to her sacrificial death. Each appearance shows the circle of the vortex narrowing.

Beauty is, like goodness, an ideal. Dostoevsky has perhaps succeeded better in creating in Nastasya Filippovna a palpable hypostasis of beauty than in making Prince Myshkin a credible hypostasis of goodness. The tragedy of beauty, however, is analogous to that of Myshkin's ineffectual goodness. It is the tragedy of the incompatibility of beauty and carnal desire, man's divine nature and man's animal nature. Instead of loving and revering Nastasya Filippovna's beauty, men seek to possess it, which inevitably results in its destruction.

More than in the case of Myshkin, the tragic conflict takes place in Nastasya Filippovna's own soul as well. She bears in her soul the seeds of harmony, love, and sacrifice, but also of spite and hatred. The tragic denouement suggests a pessimistic denial of Myshkin's dream that "beauty will save the world."

9

The Narrator

Dostoevsky's treatment of the narrator in *The Idiot* is unusual for him, though similar narrators often are encountered in nineteenth-century novels. Ordinarily Dostoevsky has a highly subjective and often a personalized narrator whose active involvement in the events and issues of his narrative cause the reader to react accordingly. Dostoevsky is also skillful at creating narrators who are alive even in a third-person narrative. It is possible that the narrative voice of *The Idiot* is one of the aspects of the novel that Dostoevsky failed to work out to his own satisfaction.[16] Some critics consider the novel a failure for this reason.[17]

The narrator of *The Idiot* is somewhere in the middle between the chronicler of *The Possessed*, who is an immediate observer and minor participant in the action of that novel, and the impersonal and relatively detached narrator of *Crime and Punishment*. The narrator of *The Idiot* never identifies himself, not even to the extent the narrator of *The Brothers Karamazov* does, but his presence is felt throughout the novel, albeit in different ways. The narrator asserts himself quite explicitly at the beginning of each of the four parts and in the epilogue and then in various different ways throughout the text. Some of these are subtle and may remain unrecognized by the reader. Thus, the narrator's presence is signaled by emphatic particles and modal adverbs, for example: "The general flushed *terribly*. Kolya blushed *too* and squeezed his head in his hands. Ptitsyn turned away quickly. Ferdyshchenko was *the only one* who went on laughing. *There is no need* to speak of Ganya: he stood all the time in mute and insufferable agony" (136/94; my italics). The introduction of such words as *even, indeed, suddenly, also,* and *too* into a factual narrative indicates the narrator's interest in the proceedings, an interest he communicates to his reader. Dostoevsky's liberal use of such expressions has been noted by many critics. In the dialogue passages, the narrator may at times disappear entirely behind simple *verba dicendi* ("said," "uttered," "stated"), or he may chime in with a barrage of "stage directions," as in the scene between Prince Myshkin and General Epanchin's servant (39–45/16–20).

In a more obvious vein, the invisible narrator assumes various specific positions or attitudes, all by way of familiar literary conventions. He presents himself as an eyewitness observing the action as it unfolds at the Pavlovsk bandshell (388–92/288–91). In other instances, he assumes the position of a more distant observer or reporter, marked by the auctorial *we:* "Here we cannot go into the details, but we will mention briefly that the upshot of the interview was that the general scared Lizaveta Prokofyevna, and by his bitter insinuations against Ganya had roused her indignation" (552/418). Elsewhere, the narrator appears as a reporter of secondhand information obtained from named or unnamed sources: "Myshkin spent a whole hour with her; we do not know what they talked about. Darya Alexeyevna said that they parted peaceably and happily an hour later" (646/491).

In his account of what happened during the two weeks after Aglaya's "duel" with Nastasya Filippovna the narrator assumes the pose of an investigator who gathers information from various sources and sorts out what he believes to be correct (625–31/475–80). Ippolit appears to be his main informant; others remain unnamed. Going one step further, the narrator appears as a tongue-in-cheek gossip monger who, not without obvious irony, reports rumors about town involving the novel's principals:

> A story was told indeed of some little prince who was a simpleton (no one could be sure of his name), who had suddenly come into a vast fortune and married a French-woman, a notorious dancer of the cancan from the Chateau-de-Fleurs in Paris. But others declared that it was a general who had come in for a fortune, and that the man who had married the notorious French cancan dancer was a young Russian merchant of untold wealth, and that at his wedding, from pure bravado, he had when drunk burnt in a candle lottery tickets to the value of seven hundred thousand roubles. (210/150)

Irony is an effective means to establish contact between a narrator and his reader. Dostoevsky, a master of irony, employs it in different nuances ranging, depending on the subject, from gentle teasing to a resigned understanding for human foibles, sardonic humor, or bitter sarcasm. Kolya and the Epanchin ladies have the benefit of the first: "This was more than Kolya could endure, when he had even asked Ganya, without telling him why, to lend him his new green scarf for the occasion. He was bitterly offended" (220/158). For another example, the description of the Epanchin ladies at lunch early in chapter 4 of part 1 has a tone of good-natured humor. Throughout the novel, the affairs of the Epanchin family are treated with the same fond irony as the young ladies' healthy appetites.

General Epanchin, Keller, and some other characters are the butt of the narrator's sardonic humor, which, however, lacks malice. Even the general's adulterous designs on Nastasya Filippovna are dealt with rather mildly: "On the other hand, the strangest and most incredible rumor concerning no less honored a person than Ivan Fyodorovich appeared, alas! more and more well founded as time went on" (72/43). Keller is the butt of the narrator's humor throughout the novel. Here he is introduced to the reader: "The sub-lieutenant promised, to judge by appearances, more skill and dexterity 'at work' than strength, and he was shorter than the fisted gentleman. Delicately and without entering into open competition, though he boasted shockingly he hinted several times at the superiority of English boxing. He seemed, in fact, a thoroughgoing champion of Western culture" (186/133). In the last example, Dostoevsky manages to get in a political barb, for a literal translation reads: "In fact, he turned out to be a perfect Westernizer" (in Russian, *zapadnik*).

Totsky and high society are in for a great deal of bitter sarcasm. Totsky's difficulties with Nastasya Filippovna in chapter 4 of part 1 are described with obvious relish, and the description of the party at the Epanchins in chapters 6 and 7 of part 4 is an angry satire. Nasty bits of innuendo appear, such as this: "An old housekeeper and an experienced young maid were there to wait on Nastasya" (63/36). Since the passage deals with Nastasya Filippovna's seduction, Totsky's reasons for choosing an experienced maid are clear enough.

There have been various attempts to put labels on the different narrative modes found in *The Idiot*. One such system distinguishes five different narrative modes: an auctorial or pure narrator who reports things as seen at a temporal, spatial, and psychological distance (chapter 3 of part 4 provides a fair example); an actualized narrator who says that he is reporting things he has heard from specific sources (chapter 1 of part 2, for example); an objective narrator whose presence is not noticed by the reader (chapter 1 of part 1, for example); a feuilletonistic mode (chapter 1 of part 3, for example); some hybrid chapters and passages that may be perceived by the reader in different ways.[18]

A rather strange narrator appears at the beginning of chapter 9 of part 4, after the clash between Aglaya and Nastasya Filippovna:

> And yet we must, as far as possible, confine ourselves to the bare statement of facts and for a very simple reason: because we find it difficult in many instances to explain what occurred. Such a preliminary statement on our part must seem very strange and obscure to the reader, who may ask how we can describe that of which we have no clear idea, no personal opinion. To avoid putting ourselves in a still more false position, we had better try to give an instance— and perhaps the kindly disposed reader will understand—of our difficulty. And we do this the more readily as this instance will not make a break in our narrative, but will be the direct continuation of it. (625–26/475–76)

Here the narrator presents himself as the "implied author," or quite conceivably as Fyodor Mikhailovich Dostoevsky, something Dostoevsky hardly ever does in his fiction. His principle was never to "show his own mug," as he once put it. A notebook entry explains this passage rather well: "However, we agree that we may be told: 'All this may be so, you are right, but you were incapable of presenting the matter, to justify the facts, you are a poor artist.' In that case, of course, nothing can be done" (276). It appears that Dostoevsky's gauche attempt at defending his idea, as it appears in the definitive text, is one of the signs of incomplete editing by the author.

Like Dostoevsky's other novels, *The Idiot* features a great deal of stream of consciousness. Over long stretches of the text, the reader is asked to follow the hero's inner life. This happens in three different ways: the narrator reports the hero's thoughts and feelings in paraphrase, presents them in the form of an inner monologue, or uses what the Germans call *erlebte Rede* and *erlebtes Gefühl,* where the subject's thoughts and emotions pass through the prism of the narrator's or another character's consciousness. All three methods may be used alternately in the same scene or chapter, as in chapter 5 of part 2, which has Prince Myshkin wandering through the streets of Petersburg just before Rogozhin's attempt on his life, frustrated by the Prince's epileptic fit. The narrator's point of view shifts repeatedly in this chapter; he slips under his subject's skin for a while and then steps back and views him as an impartial observer. Similar shifts occur in the presentation of Totsky's thoughts about his relationship with Nastasya Filippovna in chapter 4 of part 1. The narrator, as it were, slips under Totsky's skin and experiences all his difficulties from Totsky's point of view, which naturally creates some ironic tension. Here is an example of *erlebte Rede:* "Evidently there was something else in it: there were indications of a chaotic ferment at work in mind and heart, something like romantic indignation—God knows why and with whom!—an insatiable and exaggerated passion of contempt; in fact, something highly ridiculous and inadmissible in good society, and bound to be a regular nuisance to any well-bred man" (65/37). But such *erlebte Rede* alternates with passages that belong strictly to the narrator, and there is some direct speech inserted here and there. For another example, Mme Epanchin's worries about her daughters in chapter 1 of part 3 come through in a mixture of narrator's observations, *erlebte Rede,* and Mme Epanchin's inner monologue, some of it in direct and some in indirect speech.

10

The Psychological Backdrop

The Idiot is a psychological novel that poses a challenge to the reader. As Skaftymov observed many years ago, its psychological content appears on at least two different levels—a surface level that is made explicit by the action of the novel and the narrator's comments and a deeper level that the perceptive reader has to discover for himself.

Several critics have pointed out that *The Idiot* is the most autobiographic of Dostoevsky's novels. Mochulsky sees the Prince as an "artistic self-portrait" and his story as the writer's spiritual autobiography. Geir Kjetsaa calls the Prince an "idealized self-portrait." Prince Myshkin, like his creator, is an epileptic. The following scene as reported by Dostoevsky's friend Nikolai Strakhov illustrates this connection:

> He was talking of something exalted and joyous; when I supported his thought with some observation, he turned to me with an inspired face, indicating that his inspiration had reached the highest level. He stopped for a moment, as if searching for a word for his thought, and had already

opened his mouth. I was looking at him with concentrated attention, sensing that he would say something unusual, that I would hear a revelation. Suddenly from his open mouth there came a strange, sustained and senseless sound and he collapsed in a faint on the floor in the middle of the room.[19]

Prince Myshkin expresses Dostoevsky's ideas, and his experiences with the Epanchin family and beautiful Aglaya may well be an echo of the writer's abortive romance with Anna Korvin-Krukovsky. Other parallels may be drawn. A significant one is that Prince Myshkin, like Dostoevsky, is an exceptionally gifted psychologist. The quality that the Prince shares with his creator is *proniknovenie* (from *proniknut'*, "to penetrate"), the ability to penetrate to the core of a human being's heart and soul. The Prince produces a painfully intense demonstration of this ability early in the novel as he describes the execution of the murderer Legros (87–89/55–56). Throughout the novel the Prince intuitively perceives the deeper movements in the souls of the people he meets. He can understand the feeling of alienation and disharmony that overwhelms Ippolit because he himself has experienced it. But he also understands Rogozhin's murderous impulses and even Keller's petty scheming.

Myshkin reads Nastasya Filippovna better than anyone else: "Do you know," he says to Aglaya, "that in that continual consciousness of shame there is perhaps a sort of awful, unnatural enjoyment for her, a sort of revenge on some one" (477/361). It seems quite likely that Dostoevsky projected his personal experiences with Apollinaria Suslova into *The Idiot*. Suslova's reaction to being abandoned by her Latin lover, as described in painful detail in her diary and almost certainly told by her to Dostoevsky, her former lover, was similar to Nastasya Filippovna's.[20]

Prince Myshkin easily sees through the hearts and minds of every other character in the novel—except Aglaya, with whom he is in love. He detects Lizaveta Prokofyevna's goodness of heart and childlike simplicity, which she tries to hide beneath much severity and bluster. He sees through Keller's "double-think" and interprets the motives of young Burdovsky not only charitably but justly.

Often the Prince's psychological insights merge with the narrator's: "Ganya's voice betrayed that pitch of irritation when a man almost revels in his own irritability, gives himself up to it without restraint and almost with growing enjoyment, regardless of consequences" (126/86). Here it is not clear whether this perception is Prince Myshkin's or the narrator's. Other instances of this type may be found easily. Occasionally the narrator confirms Prince Myshkin's judgment, as when he observes that Lizaveta Prokofyevna constantly scolded her daughters because "she loved them with a self-sacrificing and almost passionate affection" (366/271). Also, the Prince's inner life is revealed and analyzed alternately by the narrator and by the Prince himself. Several other characters also engage in psychological analysis. Evgeny Pavlovich, in particular, indulges in some elaborate speculations on the Prince's infatuation with Nastasya Filippovna and the inner life of both parties (632–34/481–82).

The narrator gives himself the privilege of reading the thoughts and feelings of all the characters, even though he takes only occasional advantage of it: "Ptitsyn bent his head and looked on the ground, abashed. Totsky thought to himself, 'He is an idiot, but he knows that flattery is the best way to get at people; it's instinct!' Myshkin noticed too in the corner Ganya's eyes glaring at him, as though they would wither him up" (198/142). In this instance the narrator reads the minds of three different characters simultaneously (in the original, Ptitsyn bends his head *ot tselomudriya,* "from chastity"). This happens occasionally but is by no means the rule.

The most interesting challenge to psychological interpretation is presented by Nastasya Filippovna. The text itself leaves the reader in the dark on several points, though a careful reading gives some answers. Nastasya Filippovna herself provides the reader with some important points. She brushes off the Prince's offer to marry her: "Ruin a child like that? That's more in Afanasy Ivanovich's line: he is fond of children!" (198/142–43). This means that she feels that she was a victim of child abuse. A passage two pages later suggests that it was a case of seduction and not rape (200/144). The consequence of it all is that Nastasya Filippovna, a young woman of noble birth and rare beauty, is considered by society and by herself a "fallen woman" unworthy of a normal marriage.

Nastasya Filippovna's reaction to her condition is irrational and self-destructive. She will not marry Totsky (he probably would, if she insisted) nor Ganya, a handsome young man on his way up, nor even the kindly and sincere Prince Myshkin. She prefers to be the mistress of Rogozhin, a violent and brutish man with whom she has nothing in common, who beats her black and blue and eventually murders her. Why so?

Skaftymov—rightly, I believe—rejected the suggestion of earlier Russian critics who found that Nastasya Filippovna was "driven by orgiastic impulses." The text rather suggests that Nastasya Filippovna has slept with no one but Totsky and that she never slept with Rogozhin. Prince Myshkin, however, who has proven himself an exceptionally perceptive psychologist, says to Rogozhin, "Do you know that she may love you now more than anyone, and in such a way that the more she torments you, the more she loves you? She won't tell you so, but you must know how to see it" (405/303). But the text also tells us that the Prince has told a white lie before, when he told the children that he loved Marie. Dostoevsky's notebooks suggest that he was very unsure about the love plot of the novel. Hence the possibility exists that he simply left open the question of Nastasya Filippovna's erotic feelings. In fact, it stands to reason that she has none—not unlikely in a victim of child abuse.

Rogozhin has his own answer to the question why Nastasya Filippovna would choose him: "Ha! Why, that's just why she is marrying me, because she expects to be murdered!" (247/

179). He follows up by surmising that she really loves the Prince but feels that she is unworthy of him. The whole course of the plot suggests that Nastasya Filippovna is so preoccupied with herself she may be incapable of loving anybody. Ptitsyn early on (205/148) likens Nastasya Filippovna to a Japanese who commits harakiri to avenge a wrong, and it is essentially this explanation that is borne out by Nastasya Filippovna's behavior throughout the novel.

Skaftymov saw Nastasya Filippovna's actions as the reflexion of a struggle between hurt pride and guilt feelings: Nastasya Filippovna cannot forgive the world the hurt inflicted on her, and she cannot forgive herself for having allowed herself to be victimized. Her rage at the whole world and her self-laceration have become equally obsessive. Skaftymov also interpreted Nastasya Filippovna's letters to Aglaya as a projection of her guilt feelings and a futile urge to regain her purity. One of Nastasya Filippovna's letters says, "Yet I am in love with you" (498/379). The whole context shows that this is quite literally true. An analogous situation in *The Brothers Karamazov* has Katerina Ivanovna fall in love with her rival Grushenka. It may be that Dostoevsky let his heroines who have obvious difficulties in their heterosexual love life develop homoerotic tendencies. If this is so, it by no means contradicts Skaftymov's interpretation.

Toward the end of the novel, Myshkin realizes to his horror that Nastasya Filippovna is going mad. Her masochistic behavior has turned suicidal. Myshkin is also the only person who sees the suffering beneath Nastasya Filippovna's outrageous behavior. His sympathetic analysis of her condition before the guests at her nameday party (197/142) meets with no understanding on the part of others present. Myshkin perceives her predicament not so much in psychological as in moral terms: "I . . . understood the meaning of honor, and I am sure I spoke the truth. You wanted to ruin yourself just now irrevocably; for you'd never have forgiven yourself for it afterwards. But you are not to blame for anything" (197/142). Nastasya Filippovna expresses her gratitude to the Prince for his kindness, but she is unable to accept his helping hand. Her obsessive behavior continues, and the tragedy takes it course. Nastasya's moral predicament turns into a psychosis with a fatal outcome.

While Nastasya Filippovna's psychological problems are intertwined with moral questions of individual and social responsibility, guilt and forgiveness, the psychology of Prince Myshkin touches on the allegoric and metaphysical levels of the novel. Various aspects of his personality, such as his clairvoyance, his meek and forgiving nature, and his chastity, are extensions of his allegoric function as a Christ figure. Dostoevsky's realistic description of Myshkin's epileptic fit has a metaphysical dimension: "Then suddenly something seemed torn asunder before him; his soul was flooded with intense *inner* light. The moment lasted perhaps half a second, yet he clearly and consciously remembered the beginning, the first sound of the fearful scream which broke of itself from his breast and which he could not have checked by any effort. Then his consciousness was instantly extinguished and complete darkness followed" (267/195).

Merezhkovsky expressed the thought that Dostoevsky's epilepsy played a decisive role in forming his worldview: "Epileptic fits were for Dostoevsky as though terrifying breakthroughs, shafts of light, suddenly opened windows through which he cast a glance into the *light* on the side beyond."[21] Merezhkovsky also speculated that Dostoevsky's ability to merge the metaphysical with mundane everyday existence was explained by the fact that mystic experience was a part of his own life as an epileptic. The "holy sickness," said Merezhkovsky, places man into the extreme regions of his divine and his animal existence, and Dostoevsky translated this personal experience into the language of fiction. The braying of an ass in the market square of Basel and the inner light that engulfs an epileptic's whole being are equally meaningful to Prince Myshkin.[22]

However, Dostoevsky certainly tried to give Myshkin enough ordinary human traits to make him credible. The Prince is brave but not fearless.[23] He is not only pure and innocent but also naive and gauche. His psychological judgment, so penetrating at times, fails him miserably at the Epanchins' party. He is forgiving, but he does mind being called an idiot.

Dostoevsky's works have attracted psychoanalysts ever since Freud's pioneering study "Dostoevsky and Parricide." *The Idiot* is the subject of a monographic psychoanalytic study by Elizabeth Dalton, *Unconscious Structure in* The Idiot: *A Study in Literature and Psychoanalysis* (1978), which has been generally well received by critics in professional journals. This and analogous interpretations of other novels are premised on the view that a work of art is a projection of repressed instinctual energies and forbidden fantasies, sexual in nature, and acquires a coherent pattern of structure and meaning beyond those patterns that are accessible without any familiarity with Freudian psychoanalysis. In the case of Dostoevsky it is not always clear if the repressed material that finds release in the text comes from the recesses of the writer's psyche or was consciously created by him. Dalton assumes that Dostoevsky struggled with the plot of *The Idiot* more than he usually had to and therefore "was forced back upon the spontaneous images and rhythms of his mental life to a greater extent than in any other work."[24] Specifically, Dalton compares the gap in the action between parts 1 and 2 with indistinct areas left by subconscious censorship in a dream. However, Dostoevsky apparently anticipated some of Freud's insights and therefore was in a position to apply them consciously. In other words, Dostoevsky was to some extent in the position of a post-Freudian writer who could consciously fabricate Freudian patterns in his work.

In some instances Dalton's Freudian interpretation agrees with interpretations of pre- or non-Freudian critics. When Dalton diagnoses Nastasya Filippovna's behavior as masochistic, this is merely a modern term for what Dostoevsky's narrator and Prince Myshkin recognize quite clearly. Dalton's suggestion that Myshkin projects Ganya's guilt on himself when Ganya has slapped his face and Rogozhin's when he feels responsible for Rogozhin's attack on himself is in line with Dostoevsky's moral conception, stated quite unequivocally in *The Brothers Karamazov*, that every human being is coresponsible "for all and everything." It also is psychologically motivated by the fact that Myshkin, much as Alyosha in *The Brothers Karamazov*, has a talent to experience vicariously or even to anticipate the feelings of others, including evil feelings. This talent is often found in artists, and Dostoevsky himself possessed it in a high degree. When Dalton declares unequivocally that Myshkin is impotent (82), this has some support in the Prince's declared virginity but is never stated in the text. The evidence in the text suggests that the Prince's feelings for Aglaya are those of a normal young man.

Dalton's characterization of Prince Myshkin as a "magnet or lightning rod to evil" (75) and a "masochist" (80) driven by "irrational guilt and need to suffer" in rather the same sense as Nastasya Filippovna (106) is close to what Murray Krieger had said without direct recourse to Freudian ideas. When Dalton suggests that Myshkin chooses Nastasya Filippovna over Aglaya because she "represents the more potent attractions and possibilities of suffering," (79) this falls in line with Myshkin's masochism. Of course this whole line of interpretation contradicts Dostoevsky's Christian intent, which makes Myshkin act the way he acts not because he seeks suffering but because he is moved by altruistic concern for the people he meets. To put it concretely, he stays with Nastasya Filippovna because she needs him more than Aglaya does. According to Krieger's and Dalton's line of reasoning, Jesus Christ was a "masochist."

Analogously, Myshkin's mystic moments of a sense of oneness with the cosmos are explained as sexual and aggressive feelings, usually experienced in a disguised masochistic form but here in the form of regression to the primordial state of the infant at the breast. This interpretation, too, ignores Dostoevsky's conscious religious intent.

The more specific sexual associations developed by Dalton are unsupported by the text as such. The text tells us nothing about Myshkin's childhood. Hence the assumption that Nastasya Filippovna is for him "the abused mother" is independent of the text. The same is true of Dalton's symbolic topography in her interpretation of the scene in the staircase (267/195), when Rogozhin waits for Myshkin to kill him. Dalton sees it as a projection of "the child's amazement and fascination at the mysterious idea of the hidden space inside the female body and at the impressive phenomenon of erection" (113). In these and similar instances a Freudian interpretation may be treated as speculation on the way in which the writer's imagination may have worked, even if it cannot be reasonably applied to the text per se.

11

The Moral Level

Quite independently of the Christian message of *The Idiot*, a moral interpretation of the novel is possible. Skaftymov saw the plot of *The Idiot* as pride, selfishness, and vanity in a variety of versions contrasted with unself-conscious humility and self-effacing sympathy. What is mainly at issue here, he pointed out, is a person's ability or inability to forgive a hurt, an insult, or another's superiority or good fortune. The unforgiving individual is reduced to his or her own self, which is in every instance insufficient for a fulfilled life. Ippolit cannot forgive those who will survive him. Nastasya Filippovna cannot forgive the world the hurt of what she feels is a "ruined life" (71/42). Ganya cannot forgive the world that he is "ordinary." The young nihilists cannot forgive society that they are nonentities and poor. General Ivolgin cannot accept his disgrace and escapes into a dream world. The Lebedevs, Ferdyshchenkos, and Kellers of this world choose cynicism and various poses as their antidote to the banality of their lives.

On 'the other side there is Prince Myshkin, who forgives everybody and everything. He has the capacity to accept a gift or a favor freely and gladly, as well as to give freely and gladly himself. Lizaveta Prokofyevna has a similar capacity. Marie, the Swiss girl, is pointedly contrasted to Nastasya Filippovna. With more reasons to be bitter and unforgiving than the latter, she blames only herself and responds with gratitude to the kindness offered her.

The contrast between these two types is evident as Myshkin freely accepts himself as he is, unafraid to face his own image and willing to forgive himself his own shortcomings and failures, while others live a lie and conceal their true selves. Time and again, such a person acts "out of character," says or does things that are against his or her nature, refuses to be himself or herself.

In a way, Myshkin is Rousseau's natural man, and the shepardess Marie is a character straight out of Rousseau (it may be noted that this episode was written in Geneva). It is, however, symbolically relevant that this natural man is ill, an epileptic, and an "idiot." This is the Orthodox element of it: spirituality rises up from abandonment, suffering, and illness. The other characters are all products of a civilized urban society. They lead unnatural lives.

Nastasya Filippovna is the character most affected by an inability to accept and to be herself. Almost all she says and does is "out of character" and does not fit her beautiful face. She plays the roles of arrogant seductress, fallen woman, "shameless hussy," "Rogozhin's wench"—all with a shrillness and stridency that amplify the falsity. Her letters to Aglaya are veritable exercises in false sentiment. Aglaya is herself a victim of false sentiments that ultimately lead her to surrendering herself to a false Polish count and to a cause that cannot be naturally hers. The Prince alone senses the falsehood in Aglaya's voice. "You can't feel like that. . . . It's not true!" he says when Aglaya threatens to have Nastasya Filippovna put into a house of correction (480/364). The Prince is also the only one who sees the real Nastasya Filippovna behind her mask of provocative behavior, bravado, and cynicism (197/142).

The Moral Level

The verbal duel between Nastasya Filippovna and Aglaya is an exercise in strident dissonances. Both women refuse to put forward their real and better selves.

Other characters are in a similar predicament. Ganya, for example, is ruined by his futile efforts to put up the bold front of a cynical careerist. Those characters who have the gift to be themselves, though it be an ordinary and wholly unspectacular self, prosper: General Epanchin, Ptitsyn, young Kolya Ivolgin.

The Prince alone is fully aware of the struggle that goes on in every human being to be himself and to free his divine image from the shackles of pride, vanity, and falsehood:

> You must take what I say as from a sick man now. I'm not ashamed; for it would be strange to be ashamed of that, wouldn't it? . . . There are ideas, very great ideas, of which I ought not to begin to speak, because I should be sure to make every one laugh. Prince S. has warned me of that very thing just now. . . . My gestures are unsuitable. I've no right sense of proportion. My words are incongruous, not befitting the subject, and that's a degradation for those ideas. And so I have no right. . . . Besides, I'm morbidly sensitive. (381/282–83)

The Prince's discourse at the Epanchins' party later in the novel (chapter 7 of part 4) may well be read as an illustration of what he says here, even though Dostoevsky may not have intended it to be that way.

12

The Metaphysical-Religious Level

On the metaphysical-religious level Prince Myshkin and Ippolit Terentyev are the main antagonists. Although Ippolit has no objective reason to hate Myshkin, he senses in him an ideological adversary: "I hate you all, every one of you!—it's you, Jesuitical, treacly soul, idiot, philanthropic millionaire; I hate you more than every one and everything in the world! I understood and hated you long ago, when first I heard of you: I hated you with all the hatred of my soul" (335/249). There is extrinsic evidence that Dostoevsky himself saw things in this way. "Ippolit is the main axis of the whole novel," we read in his notebook (277). Kolya speaks of Ippolit's "gigantic idea" without defining it. But the fact that Ippolit's idea is apparently developed further and commented on by Kirillov in *The Possessed* allows us to identify the "gigantic idea" as the rejection of an absurd life. It is up to Myshkin to refute this idea.

In effect, Ippolit reverses what is known as the argument for the existence of God "from design": the actual condition of the world is in his experience such that it makes faith in God impossible. The conflict between Myshkin's faith and Ippolit's revolt parallels the antinomy of Christ's absolute spiritual significance and the particular facts of history, Christ's promise of immortality and physical death continuing as ever before.

The repeated introduction of the theme of execution and Ippolit's condition as a man doomed to death before he has started to live leads up to the scene in front of Holbein's "Deposition of Christ," a picture that could cause a man to lose his faith, as Myshkin observes. Ippolit, referring to the same picture, utters the ultimate challenge to faith:

> The question instinctively arises: if death is so awful and the laws of nature so mighty, how can they be overcome? How can they be overcome when even He did not conquer them, He who vanquished nature in His lifetime, who exclaimed. "Maiden, arise!" and the maiden arose—"Lazarus, come forth!" and the dead man came forth? Looking at such a picture, one conceives of nature in the shape of an immense, merciless, dumb beast, or more correctly, much more correctly, speaking, though it sounds strange, in the form of a huge machine of the most modern construction which, dull and insensible, has aimlessly clutched, crushed and swallowed up a great priceless Being, a Being worth all nature and its laws, worth the whole earth, which was created perhaps solely for the sake of the advent of that Being. (451/ 339)

The helplessness of mortal man facing inexorable nature causes Ippolit to draw some practical and hypothetical conclusions. He realizes that he could commit the most heinous crime with guaranteed impunity because his case would assuredly not come to trial: he would die before under the solicitous care of the authorities, who would be anxious to keep him alive for his trial. This conceit presages Ivan Karamazov's maxim: "If there is no immortality, everything is lawful." On the practical side, too, Ippolit realizes that every conceivable activity or plan he might consider is made senseless by his impending death. Furthermore, Ippolit reaches the same conclusion as Kirillov does, with a more elaborate argumentation: choosing the time of his own death by committing suicide is the only way in which he can assert his independence from the dumb power of nature. Like his successor in *The Possessed,* Ippolit is loath to admit that his suicide will be an act of despair more than an act of revolt. Vladimir Solovyov, in his third "Discourse on Dostoevsky" (1883), made the point that any man who becomes aware of universal evil, as Ippolit does, but is unable to see also universal good—that is, God—is inevitably driven to suicide.[25] Ippolit in fact perceives nature not only as indifferent but also as malevolent, cruel, and mocking. At the same time, he is unaware of any beneficent saving principle.

Like Ivan Karamazov, Ippolit does not explicitly deny the existence of God but resolutely rejects His world: "So be it! I shall die looking straight at the source of power and life; I do not want this life! If I'd had the power not to be born, I would certainly not have accepted existence upon conditions that are such a mockery" (457/344). Yet at the same time Ippolit—again like his successors Kirillov and Ivan Karamazov—loves life and asks why he must be so alienated from it: "What is there for me in this beauty when, every minute, every second I am obliged, forced, to recognize that even the tiny fly, buzzing in the sunlight beside me, has its share in the banquet and the chorus, knows its place, loves it and is happy; and I alone am an outcast" (455/ 343). Myshkin, a few pages later, echoes Ippolit's sentiment (466/352).[26] The theme of man's discord with God's world is made explicitly anti-Christian as Ippolit sarcastically rejects the Prince's "Christian arguments, at the happy thought that it is in fact better to die" (455/342).

Ippolit himself suggests an escape from this situation: perhaps man or, rather, man's conscious mind does not understand the world correctly and human alienation from the cosmos is due to a misunderstanding of some divine truth. It is up to Prince Myshkin to resolve this misunderstanding, although Ippolit has unwittingly found the resolution himself when he quits staring at Meyer's wall (the wall is a symbol of the cul-de-sac into which reason takes man even in *Notes from Under-ground*) and becomes involved in the fate of another human being, the unfortunate young doctor who gets another chance at life through his efforts.

Myshkin, who is specifically identified as a self-proclaimed Christian believer (423/317), presents the alternative to Ippolit's self-conscious solipsism: personal experience of a reality that transcends individuality. Vladimir Solovyov, who was the first to translate Dostoevsky's fiction into the language of academic philosophy, said, "Nature, separated from the Divine Spirit, appears to be a dead and senseless mechanism without cause or goal—and on the other hand, God, separated from man and nature, outside His positive revelation, is for us either an empty abstraction or an allconsuming indifference."[27] Dostoevsky set himself the task to realize this "positive revelation" in a fictional character. Prince Myshkin's role as a symbol of man's salvation is enhanced by many significant details that make him a Christ figure. Extrinsic evidence (Dostoevsky's notebooks and correspondence) suggests that in Prince Myshkin Dostoevsky wanted to create an absolutely beautiful character, though fully aware of the insurmountable difficulty of this task. Mochulsky suggested that Dostoevsky's artistic tact caused him to halt "before the immensity of this task"[28] and made him reduce the Prince to something closer to ordinary human stature. But we know that Dostoevsky never relinquished his plan to write "a book about Jesus Christ." An entry to this effect is found in one of his last notebooks. In surveying world literature, Dostoevsky came to the conclusion that Christ was the only character in all literature to answer the definition of an "absolutely beautiful character" and that the closest approximation to it was Don Quixote, a wise madman and ridiculous to boot. Accordingly, Myshkin was made not only a Christ figure but a quixotic figure as well, with Don Quixote a notable and explicit presence in the text.[29] The fact that Myshkin is explicitly presented as a Christ figure makes the observation, appealing in itself, that Myshkin's story is a version of the Dionysian myth somewhat redundant. The notion that Jesus Christ was yet another hypostasis of "the suffering god" was around before Nietzsche popularized it.[30]

Prince Myshkin returns to his native Russia from the mountains of Switzerland and returns there at the end of the novel. An innocent idealist, he enters a cruel, greedy, mercenary, decadent, but functioning society that refuses to appreciate his virtues. Kjetsaa has suggested that the Johannine principle of the word made flesh and entering the world was the idea that guided Dostoevsky in creating this character. Prince Myshkin is of ancient noble lineage but impoverished and a recipient of charity until informed that he has come into a large inheritance, which he claims on his return to Russia. His physical appearance reminds one of an icon of a Russian saint, and he has some pronounced monkish traits. He is a virgin at twenty-six, painfully chaste, has a love for medieval manuscripts and calligraphy, even wears a cloak that resembles a monk's cassock and cowl. He has a saint's humility, an unconditional willingness to forgive any wrong, and refuses to be provoked to anger by violence. When Ganya slaps his face he responds by saying, "Oh, how ashamed you will be of what you've done!" (142/99). Rogozhin calls him "such a sheep," and he is called an "idiot" by various parties throughout the novel, although he is during the whole action of the novel obviously quite sane. His "terrible power of humility" (an idea of Myshkin's, echoed by Ippolit) is that of the kenotic[31] Christ of the Eastern church, Christ who has divested Himself of all His glory and may appear in the hypostasis of a humble beggar.

Myshkin has other Christ-like traits. He is pure in mind and a virgin. He is attracted to children (90/57–58). He pities Marie, a "fallen woman," and meets with the hostility of self-righteous local authorities, the pastor and the schoolmaster. The many blatant biblical echoes in the tale of Marie (the parable of the prodigal son, the washing of feet, the Mary Magdalene theme) enhance Myshkin's Christ-like image. He seems clairvoyant, though his penetrating understanding of people is psychologically motivated by the genuine interest he takes in people and by his willingness to see things from their viewpoint (see, for example, 238/172 and 469/354). He inwardly relives not only all the terrible suffering that is part of the human condition, but also the evil and murderous passions that cause it. He knows very well how Rogozhin feels.[32] Aglaya at one point says that though he is sometimes "sick in his mind," he has more wisdom than all other people and that of all the people she knows only her mother has some of that wisdom (471–72/356).[33]

Before the tragic plot comes to a head, Myshkin for a moment considers to escape it all, perhaps to return to Switzerland, but then decides that this would be cowardly and that he will have to enter this world and meet the challenge that it offers him (344/256). This suggests that Myshkin, like Jesus Christ, has a mission.

In spite of all his moral qualities, Prince Myshkin is an apparent failure. He returns to the mental asylum he came from without having significantly affected the lives of most people he met. They "go on living as before and have changed but little" (668/508). A notebook entry confirms this but adds, "But wherever he did *touch* someone, he left an indelible trace everywhere" (242). The Prince may be held responsible for Nastasya Filippovna's tragic and Aglaya's disappointing fates. There are critics who understand the allegoric message of *The Idiot* to be a negative one. Murray Krieger properly entitled his interpretation "The Curse of Saintliness."[34] Some other critics have suggested that although Dostoevsky's original intent was to present a positive alternative to Ippolit's pessimistic existential philosophy, the integrity of his creative imagination forced him to let Myshkin, Ippolit's ideological antagonist, fail dismally.[35] These critics do not consider the fact that Jesus Christ was in their terms a failure: people went on living as before and changed but little even after He departed this world. Some of the most beloved saints of the Russian church were not successful prelates but humble martyrs or "fools in Christ." Myshkin's response to Ippolit's challenge has to be found in something other than the plot of the novel.

Edward Wasiolek, in his book *Dostoevsky: The Major Fiction* (1964), put it this way: "The Prince is a success because for a moment he is able to kindle the faith in others of a truer image of themselves; for a few minutes he is able to quiet, by his own suffering, the rage of insult upon insult."[36] This moves success from the level of action and good deeds to the level of attitudes of the human soul. Kjetsaa, among others, has pointed out that it is precisely this idea that answers the question as to the novel's religious message. He suggests that in the context of Dostoevsky's Russian Orthodox faith the attitude of a man's heart, his responsiveness to God's grace, the degree of his spirituality, rather than his moral accomplishments, are the measure of a Christian's progress.[37]

In a conversation with Rogozhin in chapter 4 of part 2, Myshkin brings up this topic. He tells of a murderer who begs God for mercy even as he cuts his victim's throat and of a young mother who crosses herself as she sees the first smile on her baby's face, then observes that "religious feeling does not come under any sort of reasoning or atheism, and has nothing to do with any crimes or misdemeanors" (252–53/183–84). Dostoevsky's works have a pattern of tolerance of sins of commission. His drunks, thieves, frauds, and even murderers are often treated with sympathy. They also have a pattern of stern judgment of sins of omission—that is, a lack of compassion, kindness, and forgiveness.

With his own example and with those that he reports, Prince Myshkin acknowledges the irresoluble antinomy between the Orthodox Christian's position and that of the unbeliever. Michael Holquist has defined this antinomy in terms of two aspects of time: *chronos* and *kairos*.[38] There is unstoppable, irretrievable, entropic *chronos:* Nastasya Filippovna cannot retrieve her innocence, Myshkin cannot stop the unfolding catastrophe, Rogozhin cannot escape his fate. Christ died on the cross, a son of man, nor did He stop the course of history. This is the only kind of time the unbeliever Ippolit knows, time as man's enemy, time the destroyer and the bringer of death. But there is also *kairos:* the good time, the right time, the moment of epiphany, the moment when *chronos* comes to a stop, all of which Ippolit mockingly rejects (425/318). It is here that Myshkin's epilepsy acquires a symbolic meaning. He is subject to the course of time in a real world (only Christ is beyond time), but during the moment of ecstasy before a fit time does have a stop (258/188). The experience described by Myshkin is real and not to be confused with "abnormal and unreal visions" triggered by opium, hashish, or wine; it is in fact an experience of reality quintessentially compressed.

Early on in the novel, Myshkin expresses his intuitive awareness of a reality other than that of mundane experience: "I kept fancying that if I walked straight on, far, far away and reached that line where sky and earth meet, there I should find the key to the mystery, there I should see a new life a thousand times richer and more turbulent than ours" (82/51). Myshkin's function on the religious-metaphysical level of the novel is "not to alter the course of the action but to disseminate the aura of a new state of being."[39] This "state of being" is one of communion and unity with the all, with God, and hence with nature and humanity. Somewhat surprisingly the explicit statement to this effect is made by Ippolit and not by Prince Myshkin: "In scattering the seed, scattering your 'charity,' your kind deeds, you are giving away, in one form or another, part of your personality, and taking into yourself part of another; you are in mutual communion with one another. . . . All your thoughts, all the seeds scattered by you, perhaps forgotten by you, will grow up and take form" (447/336).

This "state of being" means overcoming the separation

from God, nature, and humanity that comes in the wake of human individuation and surrender to hostile *chronos*. This victory over human alienation is easier for the Orthodox Christian, since Orthodox Christianity, taking a less extreme view of the effect of original sin than the Western church, perceives man as inherently divine as well as earthly, while Western Christendom stresses man's sinful earthly nature. To Dostoevsky, an Orthodox Christian, moments in which man's divine nature allows him to commune with God and His cosmos are a part of reality.

Ippolit, an unbeliever and a self-centered, alienated individual, is looking for the absolute but finds none because he looks for it for and within himself. Myshkin, a believer, gratefully accepts what God, nature, and men bring him because he has overcome his sense of separateness. At one point Prince S. suggests that Myshkin believes in finding paradise on earth (380/ 282).[40] However, in several passages in the novel we learn that Myshkin at one time suffered precisely from a sense of separateness and alienation: "What affected me most was that everything was *strange* [*chuzhoe,* which is perhaps better translated by "alien"]; I realized that. I was crushed by the strangeness of it. I was finally roused from this gloomy state, I remember, one evening on reaching Switzerland at Bâle, and I was roused by the bray of an ass in the marketplace" (78–79/ 48). Later in the novel, Myshkin remembers how he had "stretched out his hand to that bright, infinite blue, and had shed tears" because "he was utterly outside all this" (466/351). However, Myshkin's alienation is different from Ippolit's. It is not alienation through individuation, the inevitable result of human free will and a condition that follows the fall from grace, but rather the pristine condition of a soul that is awakening to a consciousness of self, of its freedom, and of God.

The allegoric role of Nastasya Filippovna is announced early in the novel. As Myshkin is left alone with her photograph, he raises it to his lips and kisses it (104/68). Adelaida, on seeing it, says: "With beauty like that one might turn the world upside down" (105/69). Nastasya Filippovna's is no ordinary beauty. (Adelaida, it must be noted, is herself an exceptionally handsome woman.) Nastasya Filippovna's is a beauty illuminated by an aura of the ideal. Mochulsky, who on the empirical plane describes Nastasya Filippovna as a "proud beauty" and "wronged heart," projects her to the metaphysical plane as "a symbol of pure beauty," seduced and degraded by "the prince of this world." Myshkin immediately recognizes in her divine Psyche, an emanation of the world soul.[41] In a somewhat less fanciful way, one may see Nastasya Filippovna as a symbol of pure beauty cast into a world that is incapable of appreciating beauty. Totsky, Ganya, Epanchin, and Rogozhin, each in his own way, futilely seek to possess her. Totsky, who fancies himself an aesthete, is really a common lecher, who reduces the radiant beauty of an innocent maiden to the glamor of a demimondaine. Rogozhin, obsessed with the urge to possess her, does not realize that he is pursuing beauty, an ideal entity, which must inevitably elude his violent carnal passion. Nastasya Filippovna tells him that his passion for her is no different from his father's obsession with the accumulation of money, also a futile pursuit of a forever elusive goal. Rogozhin, wiser than his father, kills her. Only Myshkin can perceive the ideal of pure beauty in her. Myshkin, who says that "beauty will save the world," cannot save Nastasya Filippovna. The very context (423/317) suggests that he was wrong. This agrees with the message of *The Brothers Karamazov*, where Dimitry Karamazov, a believer in the power of beauty, learns that it is not beauty that saves the world, but faith.

Nastasya Filippovna's beauty suffers the same fate as Prince Myshkin's saintliness. In mundane, temporal terms, it does not save anyone. It does turn the world upside down, and it causes Nastasya Filippovna and all the men around her nothing but grief. But as a vision, as the symbol of an ideal, it is an immediate revelation of the divine. Again, this makes more sense in an Orthodox Christian context than it does in a secular context.

The Orthodox belief that ideally the human face has retained the divine features of God's face, a belief on which the worship of icons is based, makes Prince Myshkin's reaction to Nastasya Filippovna's portrait more understandable.

The irresoluble contradiction between two opposing principles is underlined by recurrent bursts of strident dissonance, scandal, and violence that disturb the otherwise placid world of middle-class St. Petersburg. Prince Myshkin's appearance coincides with an eruption of disorder, discord, and ultimately misery and death in the world he has entered. This is allegorically significant. The temporal world to which Christ descended was one of discord and violence. The disharmonious world of *The Idiot* falls in line with the orientation of modern religious novels by Graham Greene, François Mauriac, Heinrich Böll, Anthony Burgess, and others.

The conjuring of scandals is one of Dostoevsky's great specialties, and *The Idiot* features a long line of them. The Prince is a party to a series of scandalous scenes. Varya spits in her brother's face, who tries to attack her, is stopped by the Prince, and slaps the Prince's face (142/99). Rogozhin's drunken crowd crashes the genteel gathering at Nastasya Filippovna's, and a climactic scandalous scene ensues (184/131–32). Nastasya Filippovna disrupts a gathering that has already seen much unpleasantness by announcing that Rogozhin has bought up Evgeny Pavlovich's IOUs (337/251). A bit later there comes the horsewhipping scene (391/291). The scene between Aglaya and Nastasya Filippovna ends in another scandal. Finally, Nastasya Filippovna runs away from her wedding. Myshkin is unable to prevent any of these scandals. Yet his reaction is in each case that of a Christian, not to say that of a Christ figure. The allegoric message of this is that religious feeling "has nothing to do with crimes and misdemeanors" or, more specifically, that the essence of religion does not lie in the successful prevention or curtailment of scandalous behavior, impropriety, violence, or crime but in a willingness to meet these acts with forebearance, kindness, and courage.

The Metaphysical-Religious Level

The same applies to a series of executions that appear in the text in one form or another throughout the novel. They are another symbol of the jarring dissonance between the principles of *chronos* and *kairos*. Myshkin brings up this theme twice at the very outset of the novel and immediately establishes the cruel paradox it entails:

> The uncertainty and feeling of aversion for that new thing which would be and was just coming was awful. But he said that nothing was so dreadful at that time as the continual thought, "What if I were not to die! What if I could go back to life—what eternity! And it would all be mine! I would turn every minute into an age; I would lose nothing, I would count every minute as it passed, I would not waste one!" He said that this idea turned to such a fury at last that he longed to be shot quickly. (83–84/52)

The point of this is, of course, that the condemned man will, if his life will be indeed spared, go back on his promise to live a life beyond the tyranny of *chronos*. He will not "turn every minute into an age" but will waste it, as most men do most of the time.

Subsequently several further executions are brought up. The Countess Du Barry pleads with her executioner for another moment of life (227/164). The boyar Stepan Glebov, impaled under Peter the Great, Chancellor Osterman, who went through a mock execution (571–72/432–33), and finally Thomas More (580/440) are brought up to illustrate the idea that in earlier days men were "of one idea" and therefore capable of making death a meaningful part of their existence, while "modern men are broader-minded—and I swear that this prevents their being so all-of-a-piece as they were in those days" (572/433).

We also hear that the Prince is "collecting facts relating to capital punishment" (426/319). There is also the description of Holbein's "Deposition of Christ," Ippolit's "Essential Explanation," and the death of Nastasya Filippovna under Rogozhin's knife. In all of these instances Prince Myshkin is more than a passive observer. Rather, he vicariously experiences each death as though it were his own, each execution as though he were the victim—and the executioner. This powerful assertion of dissonance, discord, and death is deeply meaningful, because it does not disturb the Prince's faith or his serene acceptance of the world as it is.

13

Various Novelistic Devices

SYMBOLIC DETAIL

Dostoevsky likes to use symbolic names, though a great majority of his proper and place names have no patent symbolic meaning. *The Idiot* has more than its share of name symbolism. Nastasya Filippovna Barashkova's name is clearly meaningful. Nastasya is short for Anastasia, "the resurrected," and Barashkova is derived from *barashek,* "lamb." She is thus marked as a victim to be resurrected by virtue of her sacrificial death.

Lev Nikolaevich Myshkin is a name that may well be symbolic of the strength of the Prince's humility. *Lev* is "lion" and *myshka* is "little mouse." His patronymic (from Nikolai, Greek Nikolaos) is a compound of the words for "victory" and "people." However, Myshkin is a name that is historically attested, and ludicrous names of this type were not uncommon among old Russian nobility.

Rogozhin (from *rogozha,* "bast mat, matting") is a name

characteristic of the Moscow merchant community with which Dostoevsky had close family ties. A connection with *rog,* "horn," has been suggested by several scholars who would see Rogozhin as a symbol of a satyr's savage passion, of demonic compulsion, or even of the beast of the Apocalypse, depending on whether a Christian or a Nietzschean interpretation is sought. I consider such suggestion to be extremely farfetched. Similarly, the fact that Lebedev (*lebed,* "swan"), Ivolgin (*ivolga,* "oriole") and Ptitsyn (*ptitsa,* "bird") have bird names seems accidental. Lebedev is a very common name, Ivolgin a not uncommon one.

Symbolic space is a strong presence in *The Idiot.* Prince Myshkin descends into a gray wintry St. Petersburg from the sunny mountains of Switzerland and returns there after the tragedy has been played out. It is tempting to see in this an analogy to Christ's nativity and ascension.

"Your house has the physiognomy of your whole family and of your whole Rogozhinian way of life," Myshkin observes at one point (238/172). The large, dark, somber house of the Rogozhins is an extension of the people who dwell there. It houses two other symbolic images, Holbein's "Deposition of Christ" and the bedchamber in which Nastasya Filippovna's body is laid out. Konrad Onasch has established that this scene is set in a likeness of the altar room of an Orthodox church, where the sacrifice of Golgotha is reenacted.[42] But it also may be seen as the "last room" of Bluebeard's castle. The symbolic power of Rogozhin's house is enhanced by the contrast with the Arcadian setting of Pavlovsk and with the memory of Nastasya Filippovna's childhood home, Otradnoe (from *otradnyi,* "delightful").[43]

The symbolic power of Holbein's painting is made explicit in the text. It also draws attention to another "painting," Dostoevsky's own, of Nastasya Filippovna's body laid out in Rogozhin's bedchamber.

The description of the photograph of Nastasya Filippovna early on (52/27, 104/68) is the only instance in the novel in which a human face is described in detail. The photograph is a symbol that foreshadows her fate. This beautiful and tragic face will haunt the reader to the end. It is not shown in death, which may be another meaningful symbolic detail.

Ippolit's "Essential Explanation" contains several details of symbolic force. The hideous monster that he sees in his dream and Meyer's wall, which mortifies him in his waking hours, are symbols of a spiritual crisis that renders him incapable of accepting death or embracing humanity.

The ample biblical symbolism connected with Prince Myshkin and the Swiss shepardess Marie has been discussed earlier.

The Idiot uses the device of symbolic foreshadowing perhaps more than any other novel by Dostoevsky. This fits well with the fact that *The Idiot* is the purest tragedy among Dostoevsky's novels. One senses the presence of fate in *The Idiot*. Early in the novel Myshkin predicts that Rogozhin will murder Nastasya Filippovna. Rogozhin himself says: "Ha! Why, that's just why she is marrying me, because she expects to be murdered!" (247/179) The knife with which Rogozhin kills her is shown early (249/180–81). Nastasya Filippovna herself foresees her death—down to the jars of disinfectant set up around the corpse (500/380).

The sad story of Marie, told early in the novel, foreshadows Myshkin's role in Nastasya Filippovna's tragedy. Nastasya Filippovna's flight from her wedding to the Prince is foreshadowed by her flight from her wedding to Rogozhin. The futility of Prince Myshkin's courtship is foreshadowed by his identification with Pushkin's "Poor Knight." Also, the very fact that the hero is presented as a sick man has a heavy bearing on the outcome of the plot. The exchange of crosses between Rogozhin and the Prince foreshadows their tragic vigil at the end of the novel.

Some other symbolic devices, often used in Dostoevsky's other novels, such as the mirroring and doubling of characters, play less of a role in *The Idiot* than in *Crime and Punishment* or *The Brothers Karamazov*. Although the notebooks suggest that Myshkin and Rogozhin may have developed from what was originally a single character, with Myshkin getting the bright and Rogozhin the dark sides, the actual text hardly warrants an interpretation along these lines.

CARNIVALESQUE ELEMENTS

Dostoevsky habitually inserted elements of grotesque comedy into his tragic plots. The cast of every major novel of his includes at least one character whose buffoonery develops the ideas of the novel in travesty. *The Idiot* has more than its share of such characters.

Lebedev, himself one of them, attracts others of his ilk to his house, in which a "carnivalesque" atmosphere reigns throughout. Lebedev—a petty, double-dealing "operator"—is disorder and falsehood personified. Barely concealing his propensities under a mask of obsequious bonhomie and righteous officiousness, he seems to relish lying, betrayal, and baseness in an absurdly disinterested way. He authors the slanderous squib on his friend Prince Myshkin, tries to have him certified incompetent, plays a horrible cat-and-mouse game with the pathetic General Ivolgin—all without any real ulterior motive and apparently without any real malice either. In the meantime, he interprets the Apocalypse, develops his own world historical perspectives, and indulges in Rabelaisian grotesquerie. His disquisition on the medieval cannibal who in the course of his life consumed some sixty Catholic monks and about six infants, the latter at times when he was overwhelmed by pangs of conscience about his guilt before the Church (418–20/312–14), is a spoof of scholastic theology. (Dostoevsky may have thought of a passage in St. Thomas Aquinas that discusses the problem of the resurrection of a cannibal whose body is constituted from the flesh of his human victims.)

Lebedev, in all his perverseness, is a wonderfully entertaining character, but does he have any particular meaning in the world of *The Idiot?* Curiously enough, Dostoevsky lets Lebedev, of all people, express some of his own favorite ideas. In the scene where Lebedev seeks to justify his praying for the rest of the soul of the Countess Du Barry, he becomes Dostoevsky's spokesman for an idea that is central to the mature Dostoevsky's thinking. It says that every human being personally shares in the guilt before and in the redemption through the grace of God's fatherhood—"for all and for everything," as Father Zosima says in *The Brothers Karamazov.* Hence, Lebedev's tearful concern for the redemption of Mme Du Barry's soul is, in its own grotesque way, meaningful, justified, and praiseworthy. Similar instances of the introduction of serious ideas by seemingly unworthy characters amid carnivalesque frivolity, raillery, and ribaldry occur in all of Dostoevsky's major novels. Such is the drunken Marmeladov's tearful travesty of the Last Judgment in *Crime and Punishment* or the depraved and cynical old Karamazov's challenge to divine justice on the grounds that there is no ceiling in hell to hang hooks from with which devils may drag an inveterate and unrepentant sinner such as himself down to a well-deserved punishment.

The role of Lebedev, a scandalous character, is in accord with the pervasive pattern of carnivalesquely scandalous scenes that reveal the truth of the world to which Prince Myshkin has descended. It is precisely the outrageous quality of these situations that provokes people to show their true selves. Altogether, a pattern of grotesque scandals leading up to a high tragedy is characteristic of Dostoevsky's novels.

In the first of many scandals in *The Idiot* young Rogozhin steals his father's money to buy Nastasya Filippovna a pair of ridiculously expensive earrings, and then the old man, a millionaire, grovels before that scarlet woman to get them back.

What could reveal the truth of old Rogozhin's soul more clearly than this grotesque comedy? The last chapters of part 1 describing Nastasya Filippovna's nameday party present a crescendo of scandalous grotesquerie—even the anecdotes told by the guests have a flair of the carnivalesque—with each new scene revealing the truth about the actor who has taken center stage. Many more and equally revealing scandalous scenes follow.

Each of these scenes features an individual provoked into an act that scandalizes witnesses and seems grotesquely irrational, diametrically opposed to the character's social image: an elderly merchant of righteous demeanor grovels before a kept woman, dignified gentlemen sheepishly watch a morally outrageous scene, an officer is horsewhipped in public, a retired general commits a petty theft, a bride runs away from her wedding. Each of these scenes or situations is made of the stuff that scandal sheets and rumor mills relish. From a different point of view, actually introduced by the narrator in some instances, they are also the stuff of burlesque comedy. Yet the same events are also a part of a tragic plot and a serious moral-religious argument. The chaotic disorder that they stand for is the other side of a coin that bears the mark of divine order.

POLYPHONIC TRAITS

Mikhail Bakhtin, in his seminal work *Problems of Dostoevsky's Poetics* (1929), advanced the thesis of the polyphonic quality of Dostoevsky's art. By *polyphony* Bakhtin means the presence in a text of several voices instead of the single controlling voice of a homophonic narrator. There are different types of other voices. Parody implies the presence of its subject and hence of another voice. So do irony and ambiguity. The presence of any kind of a subtext, such as in an allusion to another literary text, implies yet another form of polyphony. Bakhtin drew attention to a quality he believed to be uniquely Dostoevskian—inner dialogue carried on by many of his characters and by more than a few of his narrators. Finally, Bakhtin claimed that a Dostoevskian novel lacked a dominant and controlling narrative voice but instead amounted to a concert of independent voices, one of which was the narrator's.

The polyphonic qualities characteristic of Dostoevsky's major works appear to a much lesser extent in *The Idiot*. The narrative voice is neither individualized nor stable, but no real inner dialogue can be detected in it with any consistency. The passages in which the narrator incorporates a character's voice, such as Prince Myshkin's in chapter 3 of part 2 or Mme Epanchin's in chapter 5 of part 4, are polyphonic in a Bakhtinian sense, but they are also examples of the familiar device of *erlebte Rede* used frequently by other nineteenth-century writers—Flaubert, for example. Many individualized voices appear in the novel, but their relationship to the narrative voice or to each other is less active or structured than in other novels by Dostoevsky.

Additional forms of the other voice—irony, parody, and literary subtext—appear throughout the text of *The Idiot,* but sporadically and without the energy found in other novels by Dostoevsky. For an example of irony, there is the story of Totsky's relationship with Nastasya Filippovna, in which the narrator intermittently assumes Totsky's point of view, not without an ironic effect, of course. The Keller-Lebedev article (296–300/217–21) is an example of parody. Examples of other literary subtexts have been presented earlier.

As far as pure writing is concerned, *The Idiot* is on balance probably the least powerful of Dostoevsky's major works. Largely on these grounds, John Jones, in a remarkable monographic study of Dostoevsky's oeuvre, has excluded *The Idiot* from his catalog of Dostoevsky's great works. There is ample evidence in Dostoevsky's correspondence to suggest that the writer was himself displeased with the form he gave his idea.

Dostoevsky was a writer who was eminently conscious of

the voice or voices in which he would address his reader. His notes show him often urging himself to adopt a certain style, voice, or manner. In fact, as Bakhtin's analysis has made plausible, the peculiar polyphonic energy of Dostoevsky's texts is a cardinal factor of his creative achievement. Some novels of his that do not enjoy the reputation of *The Idiot* and are certainly inferior to it in depth of thought, wealth of memorable characters, and tragic power, such as *Poor Folk, The Gambler,* and *A Raw Youth,* have texts that are energized by the palpable presence of a vibrant living voice engaged in an incessant inner dialogue.

John Jones has suggested another point in which *The Idiot* is not a typical Dostoevskian novel.[44] Ordinarily, Dostoevsky works obliquely by indirection. He advances his argument by playing devil's advocate with his left hand and undermining and eventually exploding the devil's position with his right hand. Such is the treatment accorded the rebellious heroes of *Crime and Punishment, The Possessed,* and *The Brothers Karamazov.* This procedure is largely reversed in *The Idiot.* It is Prince Myshkin, a Christ figure, who is under relentless attack. It is he who ultimately seems to have succumbed, while his antagonist Ippolit appears to stand undefeated to the end. The Christian logic of this is flawless, as has been pointed out earlier, but artistically this scheme seems less challenging and less satisfying than what we so admire in Dostoevsky's other works.

Notes and References

1. *The Spark,* no. 18 (19 May 1868): 221.

2. No. 53 (24 February 1868), no. 92 (6 April 1868), no. 250 (13 September 1868).

3. *Russian Speech,* May 1879, 271–73.

4. *Evening Gazette,* no. 1, 1 January 1869.

5. *National Annals,* April 1871, 301–2.

6. Ibid., 302–3.

7. Published in *The Week,* no. 22, June 1874.

8. In *Dostoevsky's Creative Journey (Tvorcheskii put' Dostoevskogo),* ed. N. L. Brodsky (Leningrad: Seyatel', 1924), 131–85.

9. In *The Tragic Vision: The Confrontation of Extremity* (Baltimore: Johns Hopkins University Press, 1960), 209–17.

10. *Polnoe sobranie sochinenii v tridtsati tomakh,* vol. 28 (Leningrad: Nauka, 1972–), 251; hereafter cited in the text as *PSS.*

11. Konstantin Mochulsky, *Dostoevsky: His Life and Work,* trans. with an introduction by Michael A. Minihan (Princeton, N.J.: Princeton University Press, 1967), 365.

12. Harold Rosenberg, "*The Idiot:* Second Century," *New Yorker,* 5 October 1968, 171.

13. A. P. Skaftymov, "Tematicheskaya kompozitsiya romana *Idiot,*" in *Tvorcheskii put' Dostoevskogo: Sbornik statei,* ed. N. L. Brodsky (Leningrad: Seyatel', 1924), 133.

14. See Olga Matich, "*The Idiot:* A Feminist Reading," in *Dostoevsky and the Human Condition after a Century,* ed. Alexej Ugrinsky, Frank S. Lambasa, and Valija K. Ozolins (New York: Greenwood Press, 1986), 53–60. Matich suggests that Dostoevsky's image of the "positively beautiful individual" is a man with female attributes and

that the two nascently masculinized women are both attracted to him, and vice versa (56). Matich also believes that the treatment of the sex roles in this novel indicates Dostoevsky's belief in the moral superiority of women but lack of real concern with their social status (58).

15. See C. J. G. Turner, "Between Part I and Part II of *Idiot*," *Slavonic and East European Review*, 65, no. 4 (October 1987): 517–36.

16. Dostoevsky himself said, according to the evidence of Vsevolod Sergeevich Solovyov: "Recently I reread my *Idiot*. I had altogether forgotten it, I read it as something written by somebody else, as if for the first time. . . . It has some excellent chapters . . . some good scenes . . . oof, what scenes! Well, remember . . . Aglaya's tryst with the Prince, on the parkbench? . . . But I also saw how much of it was unfinished, hurried" (*Istoricheskii vestnik*, no. 4, 1881, 840).

17. See John Jones, *Dostoevsky* (Oxford: Clarendon Press, 1983), x.

18. I am summarizing Brigitte Schultze, *Der Dialog in F. M. Dostoevskijs* Idiot (Munich: Otto Sagner, 1974). Robin Feuer Miller, *Dostoevsky and* The Idiot: *Author, Narrator, and Reader* (Cambridge, Mass.: Harvard University Press, 1981), has established four different narrators: detached, gossipy, feuilletonistic, and Gothic. I have no disagreement with either scheme.

19. D. S. Merezhkovskii, *L. Tolstoi i Dostoevskii* (St. Petersburg: Mir iskusstva, 1901), 118.

20. See Feodor Dostoevsky, *The Gambler and the Diary of Polina Suslova*, ed. Edward Wasiolek, trans. Victor Terras (Chicago: University of Chicago Press, 1972).

21. Dostoevsky's own entries in his notebooks, where he at times recorded his successive epileptic fits, produce no evidence to this effect. He would merely indicate when the fit had occurred (usually at night, in his sleep) and if it was "strong," "medium," or "weak." He would also say a few words about his condition after the fit. However, the fit described by Dostoevsky's friend Nikolai Strakhov certainly suggests that an epiphany did in fact occur at least at the onset of some of Dostoevsky's fits.

22. See Walter Nigg, *Der christliche Narr* (Zürich: Artemis-Verlag, 1956), 349–403. The following passage from Lev Shestov, a Russian philosopher who devoted a great deal of attention to Dostoevsky, may also be relevant here: "In Russia the people venerate and

even love (one does not know why) their mental cripples. Somehow they feel that the shrieks of the possessed are not entirely devoid of meaning and that the wretched life of the simpletons is not as meaningless and repugnant as might appear. And indeed, an hour will come when each of us will cry, as did the most perfect of men: 'My God, my God, why hast Thou forsaken me?' And then we shall leave the riches we have gathered and set out on the road like miserable vagabonds, or like Abraham, who, according to the word of the Apostle, departed without knowing where he was going" (Lev Shestov, *Afiny i Ierusalim* (Paris: YMCA Press, 1951), 254).

23. See Romano Guardini, *Religiöse Gestalten in Dostojewskijs Werk* (Munich: Josef Kösel, 1947), 93.

24. Elizabeth Dalton, *Unconscious Structure in* The Idiot: *A Study in Literature and Psychoanalysis* (Princeton, N.J.: Princeton University Press, 1978), 125; hereafter cited in the text as Dalton.

25. V. S. Solov'ev, "Tri rechi v pamyat' Dostoevskogo," *Sobranie sochinenii,* 2d ed. (Brussels: Foyer Oriental Chrétien, 1966), 3:211. Reprinted from *Sobranie sochinenii,* 2d ed. (St. Petersburg: Prosveshchenie, 1911–14).

26. These passages echo Fyodor Tyutchev's poem "There Is Melody in the Waves of the Sea" (1865).

27. Solov'ev, 212.

28. Mochulsky, 350.

29. See E. E. Bagno, "Dostoevskii o *Don-Kikhote* Servantesa," *Dostoevskii: Materialy i issledovaniya* (Leningrad: Nauka, 1978), 120–35.

30. See Roger B. Anderson, *Dostoevsky: Myths of Duality* (Gainesville: University of Florida Press, 1986).

31. From Greek *kenosis,* "emptying, divestment, riddance."

32. See Malcolm Jones, "K ponimaniyu obraza knyazya Myshkina [Toward Understanding the Figure of Myshkin]," *Dostoevskii: Materialy i issledovaniya* 2 (1976):106–12.

33. The manner of Myshkin's psychologizing at times resembles Tolstoi's, as in his short discourse on life in the Middle Ages (418/313). Like Tolstoi, Myshkin always gets to the heart of the matter at hand. It has been suggested that Dostoevsky deliberately may have given his hero the name and patronymic of Tolstoi.

34. Murray Krieger, "Dostoevsky's *Idiot:* The Curse of Saintli-

ness," in *The Tragic Vision: The Confrontation of Extremity* (Baltimore: Johns Hopkins University Press, 1960), 209–27.

35. Such is the view of R. P. Blackmur, "A Rage of Goodness: *The Idiot* of Dostoevsky," in *The Critical Performance,* ed. Stanley Edgar Hyman (New York: Vintage Books, 1956), 245.

36. Edward Wasiolek, *Dostoevsky: The Major Fiction* (Cambridge, Mass.: MIT Press, 1964), 109.

37. Geir Kjetsaa, *Dostoyevsky: A Writer's Life,* trans. from the Norwegian by Siri Hustvedt and David McDuff (New York: Viking Press, 1987), 226.

38. Michael Holquist, *Dostoevsky and the Novel* (Princeton, N.J.: Princeton University Press, 1977), 102–03.

39. Rosenberg, 161.

40. Konstantin Leontyev repeatedly challenged Dostoevsky's theology as too close to secular utopian socialism, as well as Dostoevsky's Christology, finding that Dostoevsky's exclusive emphasis on a forgiving Christ was not in accord with the teachings of the Orthodox Church. See K. N. Leont'ev, "Nashi novye khristiyane" [Our new Christians]: F. M. Dostoevskii i gr. Lev Tolstoi," *Sobranie sochinenii,* 9 vols. (Moscow: Sablin, 1912), 8:151–215.

41. Mochulsky, 376.

42. Konrad Onasch, *Der verschwiegene Christus: Versuch über die Poetisierung des Christentums in der Dichtung F. M. Dostojewskis* (Berlin: Union Verlag, 1976), 152–53.

43. Dennis Patrick Slattery, The Idiot, *Dostoevsky's Fantastic Prince: A Phenomenological Approach* (New York: Peter Lang, 1983), 108–09.

44. "I maintain that this novelist could only promote his dearest interests by stealth, by stalking them, by creeping up on them as they dozed or believed themselves safe with the enemy; but in *The Idiot* he approached them head on and wrecked his book" (John Jones, *Dostoevsky* [Oxford: Clarendon Press, 1983], x).

Selected Bibliography

Primary Works

Polnoe sobranie sochinenii v tridtsati tomakh. 30 vols. Leningrad: Nauka, 1972–. Nearly complete. The first academic edition of Dostoevsky's complete works and letters. It has variants, Dostoevsky's manuscripts and notes relating to the texts, introductions on historical background, genesis, and reception of each work, as well as a running commentary. The text of *The Idiot* is in volume 8 of this edition; the notebooks to *The Idiot*, in volume 9.

The Idiot. Translated by Constance Garnett. Introduction by Ernest J. Simmons. New York: Dell, 1962.

The Idiot. Translated by David Magarshack. New York: Penguin Books, 1977.

The Idiot. Translated by Henry and Olga Carlisle. Introduction by Harold Rosenberg. New York: New American Library, 1969.

The Notebooks for "The Idiot." Edited with an introduction by Edward Wasiolek. Translated by Katharine Strelsky. Chicago: University of Chicago Press, 1968.

Secondary Works

Anderson, Roger B. *Dostoevsky: Myths of Duality.* Gainesville: University of Florida Press, 1986. Has an imaginative but sensible interpretation of *The Idiot* in terms of a Dionysian myth.

Bagno, E. E. "Dostoevskii o *Don-Kikhote* Servantesa." *Dostoevskii: Materialy i issledovaniya,* 120–35. Leningrad: Nauka, 1978.

Bakhtin, Mikhail. *Problems of Dostoevsky's Poetics.* Translated by R. W. Rotsel. 2d ed., Moscow: Khud. literatura, 1963; Ann Arbor: Ardis, 1973. Develops the conception of polyphonic composition and "the other voice" as a key element of Dostoevsky's art. Also establishes elements of a "carnivalesque" ethos in Dostoevsky. *The Idiot* is, however, not one of the key texts for Bakhtin.

Belopol'skii, V. N. "Dostoevskii i Shelling." In *Dostoevskii: Materialy i issledovaniya,* edited by G. M. Fridlender, vol. 8, 39–51. Leningrad: Nauka, 1988.

Blackmur, R. P. "A Rage of Goodness: *The Idiot* of Dostoevsky." In *The Critical Performance,* edited by Stanley Edgar Hyman, 235–57. New York: Vintage Books, 1956.

Burgin, Diana Lewis. "Prince Myshkin, the True Lover and Impossible Bridegroom: A Problem in Dostoevskian Narrative." *Slavic and East European Journal* 27 (1983):158–84.

———. "The Reprieve of Nastasya: A Reading of a Dreamer's Authored Life." *Slavic and East European Journal* 29 (1985): 258–68.

Chizh, V. F. *Dostoevskii kak psikhopatolog.* Moscow, 1885.

Cox, Roger L. "Myshkin's Apocalyptic Vision." In *Between Earth and Heaven: Shakespeare, Dostoevsky, and the Meaning of Christian Tragedy,* 164–91. New York: Holt, 1970. An excellent treatment of the Johannine aspect of Dostoevsky's vision.

Dalton, Elizabeth. *Unconscious Structures in* The Idiot: *A Study in Literature and Psychoanalysis.* Princeton, N.J.: Princeton University Press, 1978. A reading of *The Idiot* in orthodox Freudian terms, not always based on what is said explicitly in the text. Like all Freudian criticism, it creates a subplot of the novel that may be treated as metafiction.

Ètov, V. I. "Manera povestvovaniya v romane Dostoevskogo *Idiot.*" *Vestnik MGU* 21 (1966):70–76.

Frank, Joseph. "A Reading of *The Idiot.*" *Southern Review* 5 (1959):309–27. Perceptive and sensible.

Freud, Sigmund. "Dostoevsky and Parricide." *Dostoevsky: A Collection of Critical Essays,* edited by René Wellek, 98–111. Engle-

Selected Bibliography

wood Cliffs, N.J.: Prentice-Hall, 1962. A classic. It concentrates on *The Brothers Karamazov*, though.

Gibson, A. Boyce. *The Religion of Dostoevsky.* Philadelphia: Westminster, 1974. A judicious exposition of Dostoevsky's religious views.

Guardini, Romano. *Religiöse Gestalten in Dostojewskijs Werk.* Munich: Josef Kösel, 1947. Has a valuable analysis of Prince Myshkin as a religious symbol.

Guerard, Albert J. "On the Composition of Dostoevsky's *The Idiot.*" *Mosaic* 8 (1974–75):201–15.

Hollander, Robert. "The Apocalyptic Framework of Dostoevsky's *Idiot.*" *Mosaic* 7 (1974):123–39.

Holquist, Michael. *Dostoevsky and the Novel.* Princeton, N.J.: Princeton University Press, 1977. Has important observations on symbolic detail in *The Idiot.*

———. "The Gaps in Christology: *The Idiot.*" In *Dostoevsky: New Perspectives,* edited by R. L. Jackson, 126–44. Englewood Cliffs, N.J.: Prentice-Hall, 1986.

Ivanov, Vyacheslav. "Dostoevskii: Tragediya—mif—mistika." *Sobranie sochinenii* 4:483–588. Brussels: Foyer Oriental Chrétien, 1986. Has an interpretation of *The Idiot* in terms of Platonic, Christian, and pagan Slavic mythology.

———. *Freedom and the Tragic Life: A Study in Dostoevsky.* New York: Noonday Press, 1971.

Jones, John. *Dostoevsky.* Oxford: Clarendon Press, 1983. Refuses to include *The Idiot* in the canon of Dostoevsky's great novels, considering it a failure. He gives some serious reasons for such judgment.

Jones, Malcolm. "K ponimaniyu obraza knyazya Myshkina." *Dostoevskii: Materialy i issledovaniya* 2 (1976):106–12.

Katz, Michael R. *Dreams and the Unconscious in Nineteenth-Century Russian Fiction.* Hanover, N.H.: University Presses of New England, 1984.

Kjetsaa, Geir. *Dostoyevsky: A Writer's Life.* Translated from the Norwegian by Siri Hustvedt and David McDuff. New York: Viking, 1987. The best "life and works" treatment of Dostoevsky in any language. Offers an eminently sensible interpretation of the religious meaning of *The Idiot.*

Krieger, Murray. "Dostoevsky's *Idiot:* The Curse of Saintliness." In *The Tragic Vision: The Confrontation of Extremity,* 209–27. Baltimore: Johns Hopkins University Press, 1960. Advances an argument for an interpretation of Prince Myshkin as a negative character.

Leont'ev, K. N. "Nashi novye khristiyane [Our new Christians]: F. M. Dostoevskii i gr. Lev Tolstoi." *Sobranie sochinenii,* 9 vols. Moscow: Sablin, 1912, 8:151–215. Criticizes Dostoevsky's religious philosophy on the grounds that it is a "Franciscan" deviation from Orthodox dogma.

Linnér, Sven. *Dostoevsky on Realism.* Stockholm: Almqvist & Viksell, 1967. Submits the evidence for Dostoevsky's realist orientation.

Malenko, Zinaida, and James J. Gebhard. "The Artistic Use of Portraits in Dostoevskij's *Idiot.*" *Slavic and East European Journal,* 5 (1961):243–54.

Matich, Olga. "*The Idiot:* A Feminist Reading." In *Dostoevsky and the Human Condition after a Century,* edited by Alexej Ugrinsky, Frank S. Lambasa, and Valija K. Ozolins, 53–60. New York: Greenwood Press, 1986.

Merezhkovskii, D. S. *L. Tolstoi i Dostoevskii.* St. Petersburg: Mir iskusstva, 1901. Contains a symbolist interpretation of *The Idiot.*

———. *Tolstoi as Man and Artist with an Essay on Dostoevsky.* Westport, Conn.: Greenwood Press, 1970.

———. *Prorok russkoi revolyutsii.* St. Petersburg: Pirozhkov, 1906. Sees Dostoevsky as a prophet of a Russian religious revolution.

Miller, Orest. *Russkie pisateli posle Gogolya: Chteniya, rechi i stat'i.* St. Petersburg: Vol'f, 1886.

Miller, Robin Feuer. *Dostoevsky and* The Idiot: *Author, Narrator, and Reader.* Cambridge, Mass.: Harvard University Press, 1981. A detailed and cogent analysis of the narrative structure and narrative voices of *The Idiot.*

Mochulsky, Konstantin. *Dostoevsky: His Life and Work.* Translated by Michael A. Minihan. Paris: YMCA Press, 1947; Princeton, N.J.: Princeton University Press, 1967. Has a synthesis of the symbolist interpretation of *The Idiot.*

Moser, Charles A. "Nihilism, Aesthetics, and *The Idiot.*" *Russian Literature* 11 (1982):377–88.

Nigg, Walter. *Der christliche Narr.* Zürich: Artemis-Verlag, 1956. Has a cogent interpretation of *The Idiot* as a Christian novel.

Selected Bibliography

Onasch, Konrad. *Der verschwiegene Christus: Versuch über die Poetisierung des Christentums in der Dichtung F. M. Dostojewskis*. Berlin: Union Verlag, 1976.

Ornatskaya, T. I. "Dostoevskii i rasskazy A. V. Korvin-Krukovskoi (Zhaklar)." *Dostoevskii: Materialy i issledovaniya* 6 (1985):238–41.

Rice, James L. *Dostoevsky and the Healing Art: An Essay in Literary and Medical History*. Ann Arbor, Mich.: Ardis, 1984.

Rosenberg, Harold. "*The Idiot*: Second Century." *New Yorker*, 5 October 1968, 159–81. Cogent and interesting.

Schultze, Brigitte. *Der Dialog in F. M. Dostoevskijs* Idiot. Munich: Otto Sagner, 1974. Detailed and cogent analysis of the dialogue and its organization in *The Idiot*.

Shestov, Lev. *Afiny i Ierusalim*. Paris: YMCA Press, 1951.

———. *Dostoevskii i Nichshe: Filosofiya tragedii*. Berlin: Skify, 1922.

Skaftymov, A. P. "Tematicheskaya kompozitsiya romana *Idiot*." In *Tvorcheskii put' Dostoevskogo: Sbornik statei*, edited by N. L. Brodskii, 131–86. Leningrad: Seyatel', 1924. Has a sound psychological analysis of *The Idiot*.

Slattery, Dennis Patrick. The Idiot, *Dostoevsky's Fantastic Prince: A Phenomenological Approach*. New York: Peter Lang, 1983. An interpretation of *The Idiot* in terms of type and symbol.

Solov'ev, V. S. "Tri rechi v pamyat' Dostoevskogo." Reprinted from *Sobranie sochinenii*. 2d ed. St. Petersburg: Prosveshchenie, 1911–14; Brussels: Foyer Oriental Chrétien, 1966. 3:186–223.

Terras, Victor. "Dissonans v romane F. M. Dostoevskogo *Idiot*." *Transactions of the Association of Russian-American Scholars in the U.S.A.* 14 (1981):60–68.

Volodin, E. F. "Peti-zhë v *Idiote*." *Dostoevskii: Materialy i issledovaniya* 6 (1985):73–81.

Index

Allegoric meaning of the novel, 12, 42, 65, 77, 80, 82
Anderson, Roger B., 14, 95n30, 97
Antinihilism, 12, 47
Apocalypse, The, 39–40, 41, 86, 88
Austen, Jane, 44

Bagno, E. E., 95n29, 98
Bakhtin, Mikhail, 90–92, 98
Balzac, Honoré de, 46
Belchikov, N. F., 19
Bernanos, Georges, 14
Bestuzhev-Marlinsky, Aleksandr, 36
Biblical echoes, 76–77, 87
Blackmur, R. P., 96n35, 98
Boehme, Jakob, 12
Böll, Heinrich, 82
Burdovsky, Antip, 7, 46, 47, 48, 62
Burenin, V. P., 9–10
Burgess, Anthony, 82
Butashevich-Petrashevsky, Mikhail, 35
Byron, George Gordon, 24, 37

Chernosvitov, Rafail, 35
Chernyshevsky, Nikolai, 4
Chizh, Vladimir, 11, 98
Christ. See Jesus Christ
Christianity, Christian themes, Christian interpretation of the novel, 3, 5, 28, 42, 67, 69, 70, 74, 78, 80, 86, 92, 96n42, 100
Claude Lorrain, 4
Composition. See Plot structure

Conrad, Joseph, 14
Cox, Roger L., 15, 98

Dalton, Elizabeth, 15, 66–68, 95n24, 98
Death, Death penalty, Executions, 7, 32, 33, 42, 43, 61, 73, 83–84
Derély, Victor, 14
De Vogüé, E.-M., 14
Dialogue, 8, 55, 90–91, 92, 101
Dickens, Charles, 22, 28, 44, 46
Dissonances, 39, 71, 82, 83, 84, 101
Don Quixote, 20, 22, 28, 29, 38, 75, 95n29, 98
Dostoevsky, Anna Grigoryevna, 20, 21, 33, 34–35
Dostoevsky, Fyodor Mikhailovich, biography, 6, 32–35, 48–49, 60–61, 66; The Brothers Karamazov, 4, 6, 7, 8, 20, 21, 42, 54, 64, 67, 81, 88, 89, 92, 99; Crime and Punishment, 5, 20, 43, 48, 54, 88, 89, 92; The Double, 10; "Dream of a Ridiculous Man," 4; The Gambler, 20, 92, 94n20; Netochka Nezvanova, 22; Notebooks to The Idiot, 4, 19–26, 38, 44, 58, 63, 75, 77, 88, 94n21; Notes from the House of the Dead, 32; Notes from Underground, 75; Poor Folk, 6, 49, 92; The Possessed, 4, 8, 20, 31, 48, 54, 72, 74, 92; A Raw Youth, 4, 8, 20, 92

Index

Leskov, Nikolai, 10–11
Liberals and Liberalism, 3, 4, 5, 9, 10, 12, 33, 38, 47, 48

Maikov, Apollon, 27, 28, 29, 30
Malthus, Thomas Robert, 37
Marie, the Swiss shepardess, 5, 42, 43, 52, 63, 70, 76–77, 87
Markov, E. L., 10
Marmeladov, Semyon, 5, 89
Marmeladov, Sonya, 5
Matich, Olga, 93–94n14, 100
Mauriac, François, 82
Merezhkovsky, Dimitry, 12–13, 65, 94n19, 100
Metaphysical meaning of the novel, 13, 15, 41, 42, 65, 67, 72–84
Mignon, 20, 23, 24
Miller, Orest, 12, 100
Miller, Robin F., 15, 94n18, 100
Minaev, D. I., 9
Mirbeau, Octave, 14
Mochulsky, Konstantin, 13, 41, 60, 81, 93n11, 95n28, 96n41, 100
Molière (Jean Baptiste Poquelin), 38
Money, its role in the novel, 1, 9, 46–47, 81
Moral meaning of the novel, 20–21, 34, 42, 64–65, 69–71, 78
More, Thomas, 83
Myshkin, Lev Nikolaevich, his alienation, 80; his appearance, 76; the author's self-portrait, 60; a believer, 75, 80; a Christ figure, 24–25, 42, 65, 75–76, 77, 82, 92; his "duel" with Ippolit; 6–7, 72–76, 78; a failure, 77; a fool in Christ, 25, 94n22; is forgiving, 69–70; genesis, 24–25; the godman, 12, 76; impotent, 67; likened to Johnny the Fool, 12; in love with Aglaya, 64; masochism, 67; medical condition, 11; his name, 85; a psychologist, 61, 63, 66, 77, 95n33; spirit incarnate, 13; a symbolic figure, 12–13, 21, 75, 76, 79, 86; a success, 78; vicariously lives the life of others,

83–84; wisdom, 77; mentioned *passim*

Narrative voice, 8, 43, 54–59, 60, 62, 91–92
Nastasya Filippovna, an allegoric figure, 80–81, 85; is Beauty incarnate, 13, 80–81; her "duel" with Aglaya, 8, 50, 55, 58, 71, 82; her face, 86–87; her false sentiments, 70; her madness, 64, 65; her masochism, 34, 61, 64, 66–67; her name, 85; prototypes, 20, 23, 33–34; an incarnation of Psyche, 13, 81; suicidal, 63–64, 87; a tragic heroine, 52–53; is unforgiving, 69–70; a victim of child abuse, 63; and the "woman question," 49–50; mentioned *passim*
Nietzsche, Friedrich, 12, 76, 86
Nigg, Walter, 15, 52, 94n22, 100
Nihilism, Nihilists, 2, 10, 37–38, 47–49, 69, 100

Odoevsky, V. F., 4
Onasch, Konrad, 86, 96n42, 101
Osterman, Andrei, 83
Ostrovsky, Aleksandr, 30

"Perfectly beautiful human being," 6, 11, 27–28, 30, 53, 75, 93n14
Philippe, Charles-Louis, 14
Pickwick, Mr. *See* Dickens, Charles
Pisemsky, Aleksei, 21, 22, 30
Plot structure, 14, 15, 20, 22, 24, 25, 29, 38, 41–42, 43–44, 50–52, 53, 63, 66, 78, 98
Pochva and *pochvenniki*, 2–3, 4, 31
Politkovsky, Aleksei, 25
Psychoanalytic interpretation, 42, 66–68
Ptitsyn, 7, 22, 46, 55, 47, 62, 64, 71, 86
Pushkin, Aleksandr, 5, 36, 37, 38, 45, 87

Index

About the Author

Victor Terras, a native of Estonia, came to the United States in 1952. He taught Russian literature at the University of Illinois, the University of Wisconsin, and Brown University. Until his retirement in June 1988 he was Henry L. Goddard Professor of Slavic Languages and Comparative Literature at Brown University. He has devoted a good part of his scholarly life to Dostoevsky, on whom he has published many articles and two books: *The Young Dostoevsky: A Critical Study* (1969) and *A Karamazov Companion: Commentary on the Genesis, Language and Style of Dostoevsky's Novel* (1981).